Rapid Documentation
of Policies and Procedures –
The Handbook

Rapid Documentation of Policies and Procedures – The Handbook

Proven Secrets from
Consulting Practitioners for
Developing Benchmark Manuals Efficiently

Juliet M. Kontaxis

with contributions from
Eric J. Ziegler

Benchmark Technologies International, Inc.
411 Hackensack Avenue, 8th Floor
Hackensack, NJ 07601

phone (201) 996-0077 • toll free (800) 265-8254
fax (201) 996-0677

We encourage readers to email their comments and questions to BTI at:

j_kontaxis@btiworld.com

This publication is designed to provide accurate and authoritative information in regard to the subject matter covered. It is sold with the understanding that the publisher is not engaged in rendering legal service. If legal advice is required, the services of a competent lawyer should be sought.

ISBN: 978-0-578-00524-9

Contents

Chapter 4 Change Management 115

Chapter 5 Policies 123

A word about additional support for your project 131

Appendices 133

Introduction

If you are reading this book, our guess is that you are probably in one of the following situations:

1. You've just gotten an assignment to write a procedures manual for your group. You are a subject matter expert on many of your group's activities, but you've never written a procedures manual and you want to deliver a good-quality manual.

    or

2. You just joined an organization or group and your boss has asked you to write a procedures manual as a way to learn about the group. You've never written a procedures manual and would like to impress your new boss.

    or

3. You've been asked to set up and/or head up a group to develop procedures manuals for your organization. While you are excited about the opportunity, you have limited experience and knowledge about interviewing subject matter experts (SMEs) and developing procedures manuals.

    or

4. You're a consultant and your client has asked you to write a procedures manual. You aren't quite sure how to proceed, but, being client focused, you have committed to the client that you are able to take on the engagement.

or

5. You've consulted some of the other books on writing procedures and still have questions on the best approach. You're comfortable with all the tips on writing style and formats, but you'd like to learn more about the process of organizing, collecting and recording data; interviewing subject matter experts; and managing content and the overall project.

or

6. You've been asked to develop a policy. You realize that policies can sometimes be tricky to write and require sign-off by numerous stakeholders. You'd like to get the job done quickly, and you are looking for ways to facilitate the development process.

Your situation may differ somewhat from what's described above, but we designed this book to assist individuals who are committed to producing a high-quality manual or policy but:

- Are novices in developing procedures manuals and/or policies

- Don't consider writing to be their strong suit

- Are not the subject matter expert (SME)

- Would like to complete the manual(s) or policy fairly quickly

This pretty much describes the situation our consulting practice faced in 1997, when a client asked us to develop standardized policies and procedures manuals for several trading desks which he managed at a large international bank. We first asked ourselves, "Do we want this engagement?" One of the benefits of being a consulting firm is that you like to think that you can say "no." Based on the relationship with the client, however, we concluded that we had to say "yes."

That "yes" led us to design a process for developing high-quality manuals rapidly, which we will share step by step with you. We've utilized this process hundreds of times over to develop all types of manuals for both existing groups as well as new functions/businesses. We've applied it to groups operating in very complex environments. We've used it in very challenging data collection situations. Since developing our process, we've trained dozens of consultants with average writing capabilities to develop manuals.

Our process is fast and results in a superior manual. What makes our manuals superior? They're:

- Comprehensive
- Easy to use
- Easy to maintain and update
- Easy to transfer to other groups within the organization performing similar activities

Procedures versus Policies...

Before we get started, we would like to say a few words about how policies differ from procedures. In our work with clients, we often encounter confusion about the distinction.

Simply put:

- Policies are rules.
- Procedures describe how the rules are followed.

Policy rules may be derived from regulatory or industry requirements, or they may be rules specific to an organization. By way of example, public companies are required to comply with the Sarbanes-Oxley Act, which stipulates the institution of a whistle-blower policy. Many public and private organizations have travel and entertainment policies specific to their organizations for the general purpose of establishing consistent standards.

Our general practice is to separate policies from procedures if possible to simplify updates to policies. In some cases, policies do have embedded procedures, but as much as possible procedures should be consolidated in one section of the policy.

Most of the manuals we develop, especially those written to facilitate audits and regulatory examinations, refer to policies. We integrate applicable policies into our manuals in a number of different ways, which we will be discussing in this handbook.

One last word on the difference between policies and procedures: procedures tend to be easier to document than policies. Even those policies developed in response to regulatory requirements tend to require agreement from key organizational groups. That agreement can sometimes be challenging to negotiate.

Because procedures are not rules, stakeholders tend to be less vested in them. In most cases, procedures already exist. They may be inconsistently applied, which can lead to disagreements. They may be inefficient and warrant changing, which may result in some resistance. In general, though, fewer sign-offs will be required on a documented procedure than on a policy. If you do encounter inconsistencies, inefficiencies or misalignment of a procedure with a policy requirement, it's best to clean up the issue before documenting the procedure.

Since documenting a policy is somewhat different from documenting procedures, we dedicate a separate chapter (Chapter 5) to developing policies.

A word about how to use this handbook...

This book is intended to be an instruction guide, a manual for developing manuals. The book is organized as follows:

- Chapter 1 – Design Stage teaches you a few basics. By the end of the first chapter, you will have drafted an organizer for your manual.

- Chapter 2 – Development Stage provides step-by-step instructions for collecting data and finalizing content.

- Chapter 3 – Release Stage details publishing options.

- Chapter 4 – Change Management covers a key challenge in many organizations.

- A separate chapter, Chapter 5 – Policies, has been devoted to developing policies.

- The Appendices provide additional resource material.

Throughout this book, we will share our manual design and development experiences, challenges and "take-aways" with you. By the end of the book, you should be well on your way to having your manual completed!

We recommend that you do a quick read of the entire book first, before you begin applying the methodology to your project.

Let's get started!

Recap:

You are reading the right book if you are:

- New to developing procedures manuals
- Not partial to writing, similar to many people
- Either not the SME or a partial SME
- In a hurry to complete the manual
- Committed to producing a quality product

Chapter 1
Design Stage

Rapid Development of Manuals – The Secret

As consultants developing manuals for our clients, we are generally faced with two challenges:

- Time pressures to produce the manual rapidly

- Limited knowledge of the subject matter of the manual

We've developed several principles, which underlie all aspects of our methodology, to address these challenges. Adopting these "golden rules" – making them your own, living by them – is critical to your success in developing manuals rapidly.

The Four Golden Rules

Never, never start from scratch.
Starting from scratch will slow you down. We **always** find some information to give us a jumpstart on a project. We **always** ask the project sponsor to send us any document that might be useful, even if it's just an organization chart. We'll pull information from similar projects we have completed, and we'll do research on the Internet or via textbooks.

Your first step should always be to ferret around and identify any information that can help you get a jumpstart.

Always, always work from the top down.

Understanding the "big picture" early on promotes efficiency. It enables you to ask the right questions to get the information you need.

Starting at the bottom – focusing first on the details and then trying to construct the big picture from the details – is time consuming. That approach brings to mind the elephant analogy:

There are six blind men and one elephant. The first blind man feels the elephant's side and declares that the elephant is like a wall. The second blind man feels the elephant's tusk and declares that the elephant is like a spear. The third blind man feels the elephant's trunk and declares that the elephant is like a snake. The fourth blind man feels the elephant's knee and declares that the elephant is like a tree. The fifth blind man feels the elephant's ear and declares that the elephant is like a fan. The sixth blind man feels the elephant's tail and declares that the elephant is like a rope.

Eventually the blind men may be able to construct the "big picture" from the various parts. You don't have time for that – you must first see the "elephant" before you begin to collect more granular information.

Organizers rule!

Developing a flexible, resilient organizer (or table of contents) for the content of the manual first is essential. One of your teachers, probably an English teacher in high school or college, most likely tried to convince you of the importance of starting with an outline before writing your essay. You may have concluded that outlines are a waste of time. If you hold that view, you may want to re-think your position, as we did.

The secret to Rapid Documentation is starting with an effective organizer. The organizer is the framework for the manual. An organizer reduces the manual (the elephant) into a series of manageable parts that can be filled with content separately.

Good organizers also facilitate maintenance (updates) of the manual. It's much easier to modify one or two modules of a manual than a substantial part of a poorly designed manual. If you are developing manuals for several groups within an organization, effective organizers facilitate standardization of the manuals and re-use of content.

Do it once!

Doing it right the first time eliminates re-work and inefficiencies. Data collection via interviews is the key event which can create re-work. If you do not structure and conduct an interview to ensure completeness of data collection, you may need to re-interview the SME. This creates inefficiencies and may also result in a negative impression of the interviewer!

To ensure that the interview process is complete and data has been captured accurately, work under the assumption that you have only one opportunity to collect the information from the SME.

Taping interviews increases inefficiencies as the tape will need to be transcribed.

An Overview of the Rapid Documentation Process

The Rapid Documentation process consists of six basic steps. These steps apply to both the Design and Development Stages of Rapid Documentation, and we will cover them in more detail as we go along.

1. Build a Strawman

2. Collect Information

3. Draft Content

4. Verify Content

5. Modify Content

6. Obtain Sign-off on Content

The process starts with the collection of existing documentation and information ("Never, never start from scratch"). The information is used to build what we refer to as a "Strawman" (step 1). The Strawman is a starting point and is meant to be modified (or knocked down, hence its name).

The Strawman is used to guide data collection in step 2. Information is collected via interviews with subject matter experts and/or via observations.

Depending on the scope and the level of data granularity, interviews are conducted with the assumption that there will not be a follow-up interview. The interview must therefore be carefully structured to ensure that data collection is complete.

As content is drafted (step 3), the Strawman is generally modified, significantly re-worked, or scrapped. The content is drafted as a final product, although it is subject to verification by the SME.

After content is drafted, it is always verified with the provider of the information and modified as needed based on their feedback (steps 4 and 5). In most instances, modifications should be minor if the data collection and content drafting steps are complete and accurate.

The final step (step 6) requires the SME and the project sponsor to sign off on the manual. Where there are several SMEs, provide each SME with the verified draft content for sign-off to ensure consistency across SMEs. Any inconsistencies that surface should be addressed prior to finalization of the content.

Next, we'll apply these principles and steps to developing an effective organizer for your manual.

Recap:

The secret to being able to rapidly develop manuals rests on Four Golden Rules:

1. Never start from scratch.

2. Always work top down from the "big picture" to the granular level.

3. Start with an effective organizer for the manual.

4. Avoid re-work with a vengeance.

Successful Organizers Made Easy

The Manual Organizer

Unless your organization has a standard template for the type of manual you are developing, we recommend that your manual should contain at least three to four main sections:

Section	Purpose
Introduction	These sections provide a robust summary of the group's activities, in narrative format, which can be read independently of the procedures. Additionally, the sections provide valuable background information for the procedures. Readers who need greater detail can then go on to read the Procedures section. The Roles and Responsibilities section is especially important for compliance related manuals.
Roles and Responsibilities	
Procedures	This section provides step-by-step descriptions of the specifics of what is being done. The purpose of the manual will determine the appropriate level of granularity for the procedures.
References	References provide supplementary information, including exhibits, policies and other manuals.

Sample organizers for the Introduction and Roles and Responsibilities sections of compliance related and operational manuals are provided below. These samples are best used as starting points for your manual. Select the subsections to include based on the subject and purpose of your manual.

Sample Manual Organizers:

Manual Organizers

Compliance Related Manual	Operational/Training Related Manual
1.0 – Introduction	**1.0 – Introduction**
1.1 Why this manual is important	1.1 Why this manual is important
1.2 How to use this manual	1.2 How to use this manual
1.3 Intended audience	1.3 Intended audience
1.4 Overview of the Market	1.4 Overview of Group
1.5 Products Overview	1.5 Overview of the Processes
1.6 Permissible Activities	1.6 Risk Controls
1.7 Risk Controls	1.7 Overview of Systems
1.8 Models and Systems	1.8 Business Continuity
1.9 Regulations and Internal Policies	
1.10 Business Continuity	
2.0 – Roles and Responsibilities	**2.0 – Roles and Responsibilities**
2.1 Organizational Structure	2.1 Organizational Structure
2.2 Business Organization	2.2 Key Roles and Responsibilities
2.3 Risk Management	2.3 Interface Groups
2.4 Interface Groups	

If your manual is a compliance related manual (i.e., written to facilitate regulatory examinations and/or audits), the narrative sections should focus on the controls followed to mitigate risk(s). In general, the structure of the "story" your manual will tell is:

1. Overview of group – their purpose and activities.

2. Overview of risks inherent in their activities.

3. Overview of controls in place to manage risks.

Include subsections which facilitate telling this story. We'll cover developing content for your story in Chapter 2 – Development Stage.

For operational and training manuals, the narrative sections should present context sufficient for users to understand the group's activities and how they fit into the organization's overall activities and goals.

In general, the framework of the "story" your manual will tell is:

1. Purpose of the group and high-level description of their activities.

2. How the group fits into the overall organization – why what they do is important for accomplishing the organization's strategic objectives.

3. Description of the overall process (which probably involves several groups/departments) and activities performed by the group.

As you develop your manual, you may find it makes sense to modify the Manual Organizer. We have found it useful to treat the Manual Organizer as a draft until the manual is finalized. You should review the draft Manual Organizer with the project sponsor. This review is generally done at the same time as the review of the Procedures Organizer.

The Procedures Organizer

Most of the content of the manual will reside in the Procedures section. The most critical factor to consider when developing an organizer for procedures is maintainability. Procedures will change, so you should organize them so that they are easy to maintain. Ideally you will only need to update discrete procedures as changes occur, rather than large parts of the manual. To simplify maintenance, we recommend organizing procedures by process.

What's a Process? What's a Procedure?

Let's start with an example. Getting ready to go to work is a process familiar to all of us. The outcome of the process (the reason for performing the process) is that you are prepared to head out the door to work.

People get ready for work in different ways, however. In fact, you may get ready for work in different ways depending on the circumstance. **How** you get ready for work is the procedure.

Although procedures may change, the overall process tends not to change. As long as we are working, we prepare for work in some way.

Here are some other business related examples of processes:

Process	Outcome
Product Development	New products
Order Fulfillment	Exchange of product/service for payment
Customer Servicing	Inquiry satisfactorily resolved

Organizations develop products, fulfill orders and service customers in different ways depending on a variety of factors, including the business, its product or service offerings and the firm's strategy. Over time, organizations change how they develop products, fulfill orders and service customers, but generally the process (e.g., order fulfillment) remains constant. We have, therefore, found that organizers based on processes work best for facilitating updates.

Difficulties in maintaining procedures manuals lead to major losses for many organizations. Think about it – all the time invested in developing a procedures manual is lost as soon as the manual is out of date. Even if most of the manual is still accurate, the credibility of the entire manual will be questioned if the manual is not maintained. Designing a manual so that it is easy to maintain pays back big-time.

What's a Process Organizer and How Do I Create One?
A Process Organizer is an inventory of all the processes which must be performed to achieve a goal. For each process, you identify associated sub-processes. An example will be helpful. We'll use a process hopefully familiar to most: preparing a cake. The outcome of the process is a cake.

The first step in developing a Process Organizer is to break the overall process down into logical second-level processes, or sub-processes.

One possibility is:

Sub-process	Description
Set up	Everything which needs to be done prior to assembling the ingredients.
Production	Making the cake.
Finishing	Adding fillings, icings, decorations.

Note that the second-level process names (Set up, Production, Finishing) are fairly generic. They could, in fact, be used to describe making virtually anything.

The next step is to break the second-level processes down into more granular sub-processes. The third-level processes will be more specific, but they should still be fairly generic.

For our cake example, here is a sample Process Organizer:

1.1	Set up	1.2	Production	1.3	Finishing
1.1.1	Select Recipe	1.2.1	Develop Plan	1.3.1	Prepare Decorations
1.1.2	Buy Ingredients	1.2.2	Assemble Cake	1.3.2	Decorate Cake
1.1.3	Set up Equipment	1.2.3	Cook Cake	1.3.3	Serve Cake

This is a simple example, but anyone looking at the Process Organizer can easily understand what needs to be done to prepare a cake. The Process Organizer is effectively a high-level "picture" of the overall process.

With the Process Organizer in hand, it's easy to collect procedural information. The organizer becomes your Interview Guide. In this example, a procedure would be written for each of the third-level processes (e.g., selecting a recipe).

Recap:

Using a Process Organizer to organize the Procedures section of a manual:

- Makes change management of the manual easy, because processes tend not to change.

- Provides a blueprint for speeding up data collection for people who are not the SME.

Designing Process Organizers

Now that you are familiar with the Four Golden Rules, the 6 Rapid Documentation Steps, and the concept of Process Organizers, let's design a Process Organizer. To do this, we will follow the 6 Rapid Documentation Steps:

1. Build a Strawman

2. Collect Information

3. Draft Content

4. Verify Content

5. Modify Content

6. Obtain Sign-off on Content

Build a Strawman

If you are the SME, you will already have most of the information you need to build a Strawman. If you are not the SME, you will need to do some research. Look to the following sources:

- Reports and presentations on the group. These may be on your company's intranet, or the project sponsor may have provided them. For example:

    - Business plans, including those developed as part of the budgeting process.

    - Audit reports, which tend to include an overall description of the group.

    - Organization charts.

    - Marketing materials.

- Previous manuals – no matter how old.

- Systems user manuals/guides.

- Manuals developed for similar groups in your organization or for other organizations if you are an external consultant.

- Internet research.

Let's assume we are developing a manual for an Accounts Payable group. The first step in building the Strawman Process Organizer is to understand the purpose of the group (e.g., why the group exists, its mission) and the outcomes the group must achieve. Based on your research and general knowledge, you deduce that the purpose of the Accounts Payable group is to:

- Ensure valid vendor invoices are paid timely.

- Minimize early disbursements to optimize interest earnings on cash balances.

- Reimburse employees for expenses.

The second step is to develop a Strawman mission statement. Simply recast the group's purpose into a mission statement format. Each element of the group's mission is phrased as an outcome. Using our Accounts Payable example:

The Mission of the Accounts Payable group is to ensure:

- valid vendor invoices are paid timely,

- valid employee expenses are reimbursed timely, and

- early disbursements are minimized.

The third step is to determine what processes would need to be in place to achieve each outcome specified in the mission statement. Let's do this for our Accounts Payable example.

What processes would need to be in place to ensure valid invoices are paid timely?

- Focusing on the word "valid," you could conclude the invoice would need to be approved for payment by the individual or group purchasing the product or service. So, there's probably an Invoice Approval process.

- Focusing on the word "paid" leads you to suspect that there's an Invoice Payment process.

- And, assuming some sort of system is being used, data on vendors is probably being maintained.

What process would need to be in place to ensure employees are reimbursed for expenses timely? You guess this may be a separate process. Since you are not sure that the Accounts Payable group actually handles employee expenses, you decide to treat this process separately but create a placeholder for it.

What process would need to be in place to minimize early disbursements? You hypothesize that there may be a Payment Control process.

Based on this analysis, a rough-draft Accounts Payable Process Organizer would look like this:

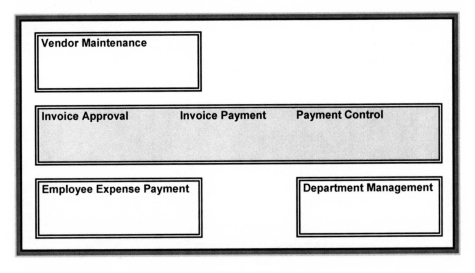

Invoice Approval, Invoice Payment and Payment Control have been grouped together in the middle of the Process Organizer. These three processes appear to be core processes for the Accounts Payable group, so they are placed in the middle (or "core") of the organizer. Note that they are arranged from left to right, somewhat sequentially. Invoice Approval would occur prior to Invoice Payment. Payment Control may occur before and during Invoice Payment.

Vendor Maintenance has been placed on the upper left of the Process Organizer. In general, processes which interface with groups outside an organization are placed around the core.

A placeholder process for Employee Expense Payment has been included on the lower left. Once the project sponsor confirms that employee expense reimbursement is handled by Accounts Payable, this process may be expanded into more processes.

Department Management has also been included, on the lower right. Any processes that apply to the entire group, such as Manage Records, can be housed under Department Management.

The fourth step, now that you have an overall structure for the high-level processes, is to go through a similar exercise for each high-level process to identify second-level processes, or sub-processes. Beginning with Vendor Maintenance, first consider the purpose of the process. You may conclude the purpose is to ensure that vendor information is complete and accurate. This assumption leads you to deduce that there may be processes for:

- Setting up new vendors.
- Modifying vendor information.
- Closing vendor accounts.

Moving on to Invoice Approval, you may assume the purpose is to reduce the firm's risk of paying for goods and services which were not delivered or did not meet specifications. You determine that relevant sub-processes could be:

- Verifying that the invoice is approved by the purchaser of the goods/services.
- Resolving issues with unapproved invoices.
- Responding to inquiries about invoices from vendors.

Invoice Payment, you conjecture, could take place either electronically or via check. Payment Control could involve reconciling payables accounts.

For Department Management, you may include a few generic processes. Employee Expense Management, as discussed previously, is essentially a placeholder pending discussion with the project sponsor. For this reason, no sub-processes have been included.

Completing the exercise results in the following rough draft of an Accounts Payable Process Organizer:

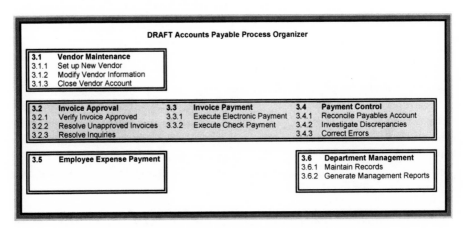

Also note the following about the rough-draft Process Organizer:

- The Process Organizer is used to organize the Procedures section of a manual. In this example, the numbering scheme for the Process Organizer assumes the Procedures section is section 3 of the manual. The first section should be a narrative introduction. The second section may be a narrative section on roles and responsibilities. If a section on roles and responsibilities is not needed, the Procedures section would be section 2.

- The convention for naming processes is:

  - At the 2-digit level (e.g., 3.1), nouns are used to describe the process. Ideally, the process is described as an outcome (e.g., Invoice Payment).

  - At the 3-digit level (e.g., 3.1.1), sub-processes begin with a verb – ideally an action verb.

Naming processes and sub-processes can be challenging. In developing the Strawman Process Organizer, select names that are "good enough." You will modify the names as you finalize the Process Organizer.

At this point, you should have a good rough-draft Process Organizer. If you are not the SME, your next step will be to review the organizer with the SME, who may also be the project sponsor. If you are the SME, you will want to review the organizer with other SMEs in your group for completeness and accuracy. Getting their participation early on will result in a more robust manual and facilitate verification of the manual.

Collect Information to Finalize the Organizers

After you have drafted the Strawman Manual Organizer and Process Organizer, you will need to collect information to finalize the organizers. Generally, you collect this information via an interview with either the project sponsor or an appropriate SME. This individual, usually the head of the group, should have a good understanding of the overall activities of the group. Let's assume this individual is the department head.

Since Rapid Documentation relies on interviews to collect most of the content for a manual, we'd like to share our interviewing secrets with you. In this section, we'll cover interviewing basics; later, in our discussion of the Development Stage of Rapid Documentation ("Conducting Effective Interviews" on page 48), we will provide further detail. The information provided in this section should be sufficient to guide you through your interview with the department head to review the Strawman Process Organizer.

Conducting effective interviews, like any skill, improves with practice and experience. This book will provide you with the basics of effective interviewing. In our consulting practice, trainees first spend time observing interviews and then gradually begin conducting interviews with a senior-level consultant present. After each interview, the senior-level consultant gives the trainee feedback.

While we won't be there to coach you through conducting effective interviews, we encourage you to debrief after the interview process. Note what went well and what you would do differently next time. If you feel an interview did not go well, zero in on what specifically did not go well, why, and how you would handle it differently. Even as professional interviewers, we always debrief after interviews. Debriefs are a powerful learning opportunity. What's great about interviews is having the opportunity to try something differently on the next interview and see it work!

We encourage you to follow our formula even if you think it doesn't apply to your situation. We've used this methodology in hundreds of situations, and it works. If we ever encounter a problem in an interview, in our debriefs we can generally trace the problem back to short-cutting our methodology.

Schedule 30 to 60 minutes for the interview at a time most convenient for the SME. It's best to keep the meetings to less than one hour. To minimize distractions and interruptions, try to avoid meeting at the SME's workstation or office. Reserve a conference room for the meeting. Always, always show up for the meeting on time.

To ensure that the interview is conducted efficiently, be sure you have completed the preparatory work on the Strawman mission statement and Process Organizer. It's critical to be well organized. You'll need to bring the following to the meeting:

- Portfolio/notebook

- Strawman mission statement

- Two copies of the Strawman Process Organizer

- Two copies of the Manual Organizer

- At least two automatic pencils and a serious eraser

For note taking, we recommend either a leather portfolio with a notepad or a notebook such as the Black n' Red type. Your notes will be consolidated into the Project Workbook (see "Project Planning" on page 26), so if you are using a notebook you will need to remove the pages from the book or photocopy them for the workbook. The copies of the Strawman mission statement and Process Organizer should be in a folder.

Walking into an interview with a pad and/or loose papers is not encouraged. It can convey a set of unspoken messages to the interviewee which could impact the success of the meeting. The SME should have the sense that you are the documentation SME. Walking into the meeting with the appropriate tools conveys a subtle message to the SME that you have the expertise to conduct an effective meeting and will not be wasting their time.

You will also need at least two automatic pencils and an eraser. These are for note taking. Pencils are preferable to pens for note taking, because you will most likely need to erase parts of your notes during the interview process. A separate eraser (we prefer the ones that look like pens, such as the Pentel ClicEraser) is generally more efficient to use than the eraser on the inside of an automatic pencil. We recommend automatic pencils rather than Number 2 pencils, because automatic pencils look more professional. The second pencil is for back-up purposes. We also recommend having a carrying case for the pencils and eraser, especially if you are not using a portfolio which accommodates pencils.

In selecting interview tools, also consider your working environment. If, for example, pocket protectors are popular in your organization, you will probably want to use a pocket protector for your pencils rather than an expensive Italian leather pen case.

Before we discuss the structure of the interview, note that the interview is a process you must control. Controlling the interview promotes efficiency. Uncontrolled interviews generally result in incomplete and/or inaccurate data collection, requiring additional interviews. Uncontrolled interviews can also impact your reputation as an interviewer. When you are forced to go back to the SME to collect data you should have collected in the first interview, the SME may push back.

It's relatively easy to control the interview when:

- You've done your homework – in this case, you have a Strawman mission statement and Process Organizer.
- You appear well organized – all the needed tools are at hand.
- You follow the Interviewing Process outlined below.

Data collection interviews should generally follow the Interviewing Process shown in the following diagram. The process consists of a brief introduction (step 1), data collection (steps 2 through 4) and a wrap-up (steps

5 through 6). Most of the time will be spent on the data collection steps, which should be repeated for each question or logical group of questions.

The Interviewing Process

1. Introduce purpose of meeting
2. Ask questions
3. Confirm understanding
4. Modify your notes
5. Confirm completeness
6. Review next steps

The first minute or two of the interview should be used to introduce yourself and the purpose of the project and the meeting. If the department head does not have any questions about the purpose, confirm the scheduled time allotment for the interview. This avoids surprise early departures by the interviewee. Depending on the interviewee and your relationship, you may want to begin by investing in a minute of small talk.

Next, ask your questions. Depending on the interview, it's best to confirm your understanding of the answer after each question or after a few questions. This practice gives you a chance to review your notes and make sure that that you have captured data correctly. This also gives the SME the opportunity to provide additional information, if necessary.

At the end of the interview, summarize the data you have collected. The purpose of the summary is to check completeness of the data. You and/or the SME may have missed critical data.

Let's take a look at the interview of the Accounts Payable department head/SME.

1. Begin the interview process by introducing yourself with a handshake, if appropriate. Thank the interviewee for their time. Review the purpose of the project, including how the manual will be used. Discussing the purpose is especially important if

the department head is not the project sponsor. Confirm that the interview should take no more than one hour.

2. After the introduction, have your Strawman mission statement in front of you and ask the department head to describe the mission of the Accounts Payable group. Check whether the department head's description agrees with your Strawman mission statement. Document any differences on the Strawman mission statement.

The Mission of the Accounts Payable group is to ensure:

- valid vendor invoices are paid timely,

- valid employee expenses are reimbursed timely, and

- early disbursements are minimized.

---

3. If the department head does not mention minimizing early disbursements or paying employee expenses, ask whether minimizing early disbursements is part of their mission and whether the group handles employee expenses.

4. Confirm your understanding of the group's mission by summarizing what the department head has said:

    So, your group is responsible for ensuring that vendor invoices are paid accurately and timely. Is that correct?

    If your notes differ from the description of the mission which the SME is confirming, modify your notes accordingly.

5. Next, ask the department head to describe what the group does, and document the answers. Listen for agreement with the processes on the Strawman Process Organizer.

    The department head may respond:

    Well, we receive invoices through the mail and electronically and review them for completeness. We determine who needs to approve the invoice and send it to them for approval. Once we receive the approved invoice, it gets paid.

6. Summarize what the SME has told you and feed it back for confirmation:

    So, the group first ensures the invoice is approved and then executes payment?

7. If the department head agrees with your summary, and what you are hearing agrees substantially with the Strawman Process Organizer, introduce the Process Organizer to the department head as follows:

    Before our meeting today, we conducted some research and drafted an organizer we thought might summarize your group's key processes. This is the draft – it's essentially a picture of what your group does and will be used to organize your group's procedures. I'd like to review it with you and see whether it makes sense.

    - Review the high-level processes first, starting with the core processes: Invoice Approval, Invoice Payment, Payment Control, etc.

    - Ask whether there are any major processes missing from the Process Organizer.

    - Confirm:

      So, this organizer is representative of your group's various functions?

    - If the department head has additions to the organizer, verify that the additions are not sub-processes on the organizer. Then, ask the department head to describe the process at a summary level, and note key sub-processes.

8. After obtaining agreement on the high-level processes, review the sub-processes for each high-level process. Expect to:

    - Delete some sub-processes

    - Modify the names of some sub-processes

    - Include additional sub-processes

9. After obtaining agreement on the sub-processes, review the Process Organizer at a 2-digit level and review each of the sub-processes with the department head to confirm completeness and accuracy.

10. Introduce the Manual Organizer, and review the sections first. Upon the department head's agreement, review the subsections for each section. Note any additions, deletions, or modifications.

11. Indicate that the next step is to re-draft the Manual Organizer and Process Organizer based on your meeting and send the revised organizers to the department head for review.

Draft the Organizers

Depending on the extent of changes the SME has suggested for the organizers, this step can either be fairly straightforward or require some analysis. If the department head has added new processes or sub-processes, you'll need to determine how to fit them into the Process Organizer and select names for the processes, following the naming conventions outlined earlier.

If, for example, the SME confirmed that the group handles the payment of employee expenses, they may have provided you with the following data:

We receive employee expense reports electronically after they have been approved by management. We review the expense items on the report to ensure that they comply with our internal policies. If any items do not comply, we reject the report and it goes back to the approving manager. Once we determine that all items on a report are valid and within guidelines, we check for completeness and approve it for payment. Our system interfaces with our Payroll System. Payment occurs via the Payroll System. We also handle inquiries from employees.

Based on your analysis, you update the draft Process Organizer as follows:

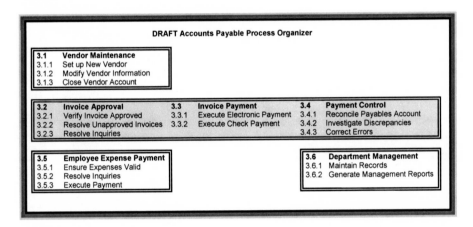

Verify the Updated Organizers

If the organizers do not require major changes, you can email the revised organizer drafts to the SME for approval. If you have made substantial changes to either the Manual Organizer or the Process Organizer, it's best to meet with the SME again.

In general, any further modifications should be minor at this point. If that's the case, obtain sign-off from the SME. The request for sign-off and the SME sign-off on the organizers tend to be "soft" (e.g., "Are you OK with the organizers?"). The SME should understand that the organizers may be modified during or after collection of procedural data. All you need at this point is agreement from the SME that it's OK to proceed with collection of data. The organizers should be labeled "draft" until final sign-off on the manual.

Modify the Updated Organizers

This step is rarely required for organizers. If any modifications are required, however, they should generally be edits of process names or additions of sub-processes to a high-level process on the Process Organizer. At this point, you will generally not be adding new high-level processes. If during the verification step you identify an additional high-level process, it's best to work through all the associated sub-processes at the verification meeting with the SME.

Obtain Sign-off on the Organizers

If the organizers required additional minor modifications, email the modified organizers to the SME and ask them to verify that the revised organizers are OK. Refer to "Verify the Updated Organizers" on page 23.

Now that you have good draft organizers in hand, you're ready to get the project rolling. Before you head out to collect procedural data from the SMEs, you'll first need to set up a few tools to ensure the project runs smoothly.

Recap:

Follow the **6 Rapid Documentation Steps** for developing content to build effective Process Organizers. These are the same six steps you'll be using to collect procedural data from SMEs.

   1. Build a Strawman

   2. Collect Information

   3. Draft Content

   4. Verify Content

   5. Modify Content

   6. Obtain Sign-off on Content

Step 2, Collect Information, requires you to interview the SME. Following the **Interviewing Process** will result in efficient, complete data collection:

   1. Introduce purpose of meeting

   2. Ask question(s)

   3. Confirm understanding

   4. Modify your notes

   5. Confirm completeness

   6. Review next steps

Project Planning

Congratulations! You've completed the Design Stage of the project and are now ready to begin collecting procedural data. Before you head out, we recommend you put files, trackers, and a project plan into place. You also need to plan the project introduction.

Project Tools – Files

The Project Workbook will be your central repository for notes, as well as hard copy documents you collect from the SMEs. We have found that three-ring loose-leaf binders work well. In our Project Workbooks, we set up sections with the following tabs:

Tab	Purpose
Meeting Notes	Any handwritten notes from interviews with SMEs or interface groups.
Research	Printouts from any Internet research done for introductory sections (such as research on marketplace or industry groups).
Process Organizer	Drafts and marked-up copies of the Process Organizer from the meetings with the SME.
Introduction	Drafts and marked-up copies of the introductory sections from meetings with SMEs and interface groups.
Procedures	Drafts and marked-up copies of the procedures from meetings with the SMEs.
Emails	Project-related emails, particularly emails containing comments or contact information.
Verified Sections	Any document (including email) with a sign-off on it from the SMEs.

Tab	Purpose
References	Exhibits, policies, regulations or other reference material to be incorporated into the manual.
Trackers	Meetings Tracker, Document Tracker, project plans, etc. (which will be discussed in the following sections).

We also set up electronic project folders, including a main project folder and several sub-folders, on shared drives. We generally save all electronic draft files until the draft is finalized. We use the date as part of the draft file name. We have found that we often need to go back to prior drafts.

For the Process Organizer you already developed, the electronic file directory might look like this:

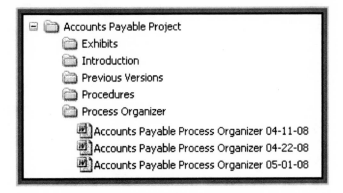

Project Tools – Trackers

It's important to track meetings and documents, especially documents you collect from SMEs that need to be returned.

To track meetings, we use a Meetings Tracker spreadsheet to track the following information:

- Date
- Time

- Type of Contact (i.e., phone call, data collection, verification)
- Who (primary person meeting is set up with)
- Phone # or Email (of primary person)
- Group or Department (of primary person)
- Attendees
- Follow Up Date
- Notes

The Meetings Tracker is useful for:

- Centralizing the names, phone numbers/email addresses and locations of all SMEs you'll need to interview
- Tracking scheduled meetings with the SMEs
- Tracking cancelled meetings (should be shown in red on the tracker)
- Recording outstanding items (e.g., exhibits, reports the SME indicated they would send to you)

Meetings Tracker Template:

Contact / Meetings Table								
Date	Time	Type of Contact	Who	Phone #	Group	Attendees	Follow Up Date	Notes

We also use a spreadsheet to track documents received over the course of the project.   The Document Tracker spreadsheet tracks the following information:

- Type of Document (i.e., book, binder, bound presentation)
- Document Title
- Date Received
- Received From
- Date Returned (if necessary)

- Returned To (if necessary)

The Document Tracker helps:

- Identify who provided a document
- Track when the document was received
- Track whether the document needs to be returned and when

Document Tracker Template:

Document Tracking Table					
Type	Document Title	Received	From	Returned	To

Project Plan

At this point, you should have a good sense of the scope of the project. We recommend establishing a project plan, including a schedule. This may require modification during the project, but it is important to have targets. You can create a project plan using a formal project-planning tool, such as Microsoft Project, or simply by creating a table in a word-processing or spreadsheet program.

Sample Project Plan:

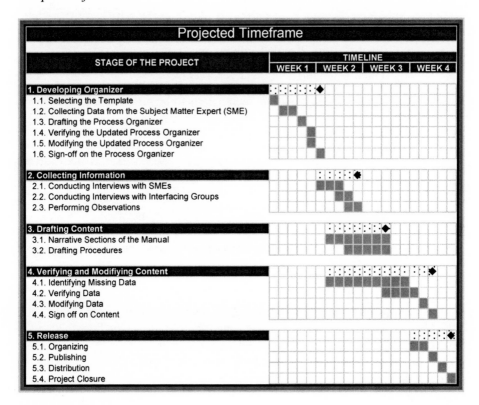

Projected Timeframe				
STAGE OF THE PROJECT	**TIMELINE**			
	WEEK 1	WEEK 2	WEEK 3	WEEK 4
1. Developing Organizer				
1.1. Selecting the Template				
1.2. Collecting Data from the Subject Matter Expert (SME)				
1.3. Drafting the Process Organizer				
1.4. Verifying the Updated Process Organizer				
1.5. Modifying the Updated Process Organizer				
1.6. Sign-off on the Process Organizer				
2. Collecting Information				
2.1. Conducting Interviews with SMEs				
2.2. Conducting Interviews with Interfacing Groups				
2.3. Performing Observations				
3. Drafting Content				
3.1. Narrative Sections of the Manual				
3.2. Drafting Procedures				
4. Verifying and Modifiying Content				
4.1. Identifying Missing Data				
4.2. Verifying Data				
4.3. Modifying Data				
4.4. Sign off on Content				
5. Release				
5.1. Organizing				
5.2. Publishing				
5.3. Distribution				
5.4. Project Closure				

Project Introduction

Before setting up the project tools, or shortly after, schedule a meeting with the project sponsor to plan for the project kick-off. If the project sponsor is the individual who will sign off on the Manual Organizer and the Process Organizer, you can discuss the project kick-off at the sign-off meeting.

The purpose of this discussion is to determine how best to introduce the project to all the SMEs who will be interviewed, as well as to other stakeholders. Depending on the nature of the project, an email introduction to the project may suffice. If the project will have an impact on many people, however, a kick-off meeting to introduce the project may be best.

At the meeting with the project sponsor, obtain the names of the SMEs. Have the Manual Organizer and the Process Organizer with you, and go through the key sections of the organizers to identify contact names. All these people should be included on the project introduction email or in the project kick-off meeting.

The kick-off email or meeting is your authorization to conduct the project. For this reason, it is important that the project sponsor send the kick-off email or host the kick-off meeting. The email or meeting aligns the project with the project sponsor's (and by default the organizational) goals. Proceeding with the project without the project sponsor's formal authorization generally leads to problems. The success of the project depends on the cooperation of the SMEs, all of whom have other priorities. Do not rely on your relationships with the SMEs, your perceived charm or personal power for success. All of these are important but not sufficient for success. You must absolutely insist on the project sponsor's written authorization.

Whether you decide to introduce the project with a kick-off email or meeting, it's important to cover:

- The purpose of the project

- How the project will be conducted

Now, you're ready to begin developing content for the manual.

Recap:

Setting up a project plan, files, and meeting and document trackers will facilitate the project.

Before you begin collecting information from SMEs, it's imperative that the project sponsor introduce the project to the SMEs via a kick-off meeting or an email. We strongly recommend holding off interviews with SMEs until after the formal introduction of the project.

Chapter 2
Development Stage

Overview

At this point, you've completed what we consider the most important and difficult part of developing the manual: drafting the organizers for the manual and the procedures.

You've applied the Four Golden Rules:

1. Never, never start from scratch.

2. Always, always work from the top down.

3. Organizers rule!

4. Do it once!

Your project tools are in place, and you've officially kicked off the project, either via a meeting hosted by the project sponsor or via an email introduction.

Now you're ready to begin collecting content for the manual. While this may seem like the difficult part of the project, content collection is actually fairly straightforward because you have already drafted the Manual Organizer and the Process Organizer.

We like to use a "bucket" analogy to describe the Development Stage. Every entry in the draft Manual Organizer and the draft Process Organizer is a bucket. Each bucket now needs to be filled with content. Filling a bucket is much easier to manage than filling a swimming pool! We can select which buckets to fill first and determine how they will be filled.

As you collect content for each bucket of the manual, you follow the same 6 Rapid Documentation Steps you used to build the Process Organizer:

1.   Build a Strawman

2.   Collect Information

3.   Draft Content

4.   Verify Content

5.   Modify Content

6.   Obtain Sign-off on Content

Following the "never start from scratch" rule, you start the content development process by building a Strawman (step 1) based on the documented information you have collected. As with the Strawman Process Organizer, this Strawman is meant to be a starting point for developing content and is intended to be modified.

With the Strawman in hand, you'll begin interviewing SMEs to collect content (step 2). Much of the content will be procedural and more detailed, so effective note taking will be critical. We'll share with you some of our approaches to taking notes. During our discussion of the development of the Process Organizer, we introduced some key aspects to conducting effective interviews. Now we'll dig deeper into the interview process and share our techniques for collecting large amounts of data efficiently.

Drafting content (step 3) covers the process of modifying the Strawman and writing content. You draft the content as a final product, although it is subject to verification by the SME. Our discussion of drafting content will include details of the writing structure and style we use.

After you've drafted content based on the information from the SME, you verify the draft with the SME (step 4). The goal is to provide the SME with a final draft for verification, but you may need to modify the content (step 5), depending on the complexity and granularity of the data.

The final step (step 6) requires sign-off by the SME and the project sponsor. In situations where there are several SMEs, you provide all SMEs with the verified draft content for sign-off to ensure consistency across SMEs. Any inconsistencies that surface should be addressed prior to finalization of the content.

Let's get started on developing content!

Recap:

Developing content for the manual follows the same 6 Rapid Documentation Steps you used to build the Process Organizer:

1. Build a Strawman

2. Collect Information

3. Draft Content

4. Verify Content

5. Modify Content

6. Obtain Sign-off on Content

In the next several sections, we'll be tailoring the 6 Rapid Documentation Steps for content development and providing additional techniques for conducting efficient interviews and collecting large amounts of data.

Step 1: Build a Strawman

Why build a Strawman first for the manual content? Why not just talk to the SMEs and get all the data for the manual? If you and the SMEs have plenty of free time in your work schedules and/or there's no deadline for the manual, that could be a workable approach. For most of us, time is a limited resource. We have deadlines to meet. Using a Strawman improves our productivity (and in most cases organizational productivity) by:

- Recycling existing data
- Identifying gaps in data
- Enabling us to conduct interviews more efficiently

Building the Strawman is a four-step process:

1. Build the shell for the content.
2. Collect preliminary content.
3. Populate the Strawman with content.
4. Identify gaps in content.

The Rapid Documentation process is similar to building and furnishing a house. The Design Stage equates to the architectural plan for a house. Once we have a plan in hand, we can build and furnish the house (the Development Stage).

Building the Shell for the Content

During the Design Stage of the project, you finalized the draft organizers for the manual and the procedures. The draft Manual Organizer will be the table of contents for your manual.

If your organization does not have a standard template for manuals, you'll need to select templates for the introductory sections and the Procedures section of your manual.

Use the selected templates to build out the shell for the manual. The shell includes:

- Title page
- Table of contents
- Numbered sections including procedures without any content

At the beginning of each procedure page, we recommend including some header fields to identify important summary information for that procedure. For example, you may want to identify the responsible party, timing, systems used, etc. The header fields can vary, depending on the department and type of manual being written.

Sample Procedure Page with Header Fields:

3.1	Vendor Maintenance
3.1.1	Set up New Vendor

Responsibility:
Involved Parties:
System(s):
Procedures:

As you are building the shell, be sure to apply any applicable heading styles in your word-processing program to section and procedure headings, so that you can create an automatic table of contents for your document.

It's important that the shell is in the final format. Later, as you collect data, you may add or remove a section. Changing the template or format of the manual, however, will lead to inefficiencies. Think of the shell as a house – you don't want to be pulling down walls as you are moving in the furniture.

It's important to identify each page of the manual as a draft until the project sponsor has signed off on the manual. In setting up the shell, we add

"Draft" to the document header. We also include the current date in the header to facilitate tracking of versions.

You'll find an example of the standard template we use for a shell in Appendix 1: Sample Shell Manual.

Collecting Preliminary Content

It's best to establish a time budget up front for conducting research (e.g., ½ to 1 day). The budget will depend on a variety of factors, including the scope of the manual and time constraints of SMEs. We have found that it's fairly easy to waste time on research. At some point, the research effort yields diminishing returns and it is easier to get data by interviewing the SMEs. A budget for conducting research compels you to assess the value of continued research.

Begin with the information you have already collected. In building the Process Organizer, you collected information from numerous internal and external sources and from your own research. Review these documents first.

General sources of information include:

- The project sponsor.

- Support and control departments, such as Internal Audit, Risk Management groups, Business Continuity Planning (BCP) or Disaster Planning, Strategic Planning, Marketing Support, and Performance Improvement.

- Information Technology groups – specifically their systems development departments.

- The company's intranet.

- The Internet.

Your objective is to locate all information that could fit into your Manual Organizer, including information for the Introduction and Procedures sections. Look for any type of general information about the group, as well as specific information, including:

- Organization charts detailing the structure of the group and how the group fits into the overall organization.

- Documents which provide an overview of the group, such as strategic plans, audit reports, marketing brochures and material on the firm's intranet.

- Systems user manuals, as well as flowcharts prepared by Audit, Systems Development and/or Performance Improvement.

- Procedures prepared by BCP or Disaster Planning, other groups that interface with the group you are documenting, groups utilizing the same systems, or similar groups; or procedures available on the Internet for other organizations (e.g., some universities publish their procedures on the Internet).

As you collect hard copy documents from internal sources, update the Document Tracker.

The Internet is a phenomenal resource for material for your Strawman. If you are developing documentation for a generic group, such as Accounts Payable, you'll be able to find extensive materials on the Internet, including in some cases generic procedures. These procedures can be utilized as a starting point for your procedures.

If your manual is for a specialized group, there is generally an industry or trade group which represents the specialty. Industry group websites are often rich in information that can be useful for the introductory sections of your manual, especially to provide an overview of the industry or specialty.

As you collect documents and conduct research, review the material and assess its applicability for incorporation into your Strawman. If the information appears to be applicable, begin integrating it into the Strawman.

Populating the Strawman with Content

After you decide which content is applicable to the manual, determine where the content fits best. Ask yourself:

- Is this type of content better suited for the introductory narrative sections of the manual or the Procedures section?

- Which narrative or procedural section does it best fit with?

If you are not sure where the content fits best, house it temporarily where it seems to make sense. The goal for this part of manual development is to put all seemingly relevant content somewhere in the manual. Later, you can determine whether the content should actually be included in the final cut of the manual and, if so, where the content fits best.

Don't be too concerned with editing or wordsmithing the content at this time. You'll do that later. Again, the purpose is to pull all relevant content into the Manual Organizer.

Identifying Gaps in Content

After you have completed populating the manual with content you have sourced from other documents or via research, look through the manual for subsections with no content. If it makes sense to conduct further research for potential content, go ahead. If it does not make sense to conduct further research, then add some bullet points around what you think might be key aspects of the topic or procedure, based on your knowledge and experience. In the case of the Accounts Payable manual, you may find that you have no content for the Risk Control subsection in the introduction. Based on the Process Organizer and your general knowledge, you conclude that you would probably want to include high-level summaries of:

- The approval process for invoices
- Controls around payments

You record these bullet points under the Risk Control subsection of the manual as shown below:

1.8 Risk Controls

- The approval process for invoices
- Controls around payments

It's important to have some content for each of the procedures before you begin the interview process. If you're missing content for a procedure, it's fairly easy to develop preliminary content. Most procedures follow a basic model:

Input
↓
Value-add steps
↓
Output

For the Accounts Payable example, let's assume you have no content for Set up New Vendor. Thinking through what might be involved in setting up a new vendor before the interview will greatly facilitate the interview process. So, based on the procedures model just described and general knowledge, you add bullet points with preliminary content to this section.

Sample Procedure Page with Preliminary Content:

3.1	Vendor Maintenance

3.1.1	Set up New Vendor

Responsibility:
Involved Parties:
System(s):
Procedures:

- How is information about new vendors received by AP? (Input)
  - Memo; email

- What information does AP need to set up a new vendor? (Input)

- Is there an approval process for new vendors? (Value add)

- How do they capture new vendor static data on their system? (Value add)

- Does anyone need to be advised of the setup? (Output)

- Must any documents be filed? (Output)

Once you have identified all content gaps and added some content to each subsection, you're ready to begin the interview phase of the manual development project.

Recap:

Never, never start from scratch! Build a Strawman for the manual content before you begin interviewing SMEs. This will substantially increase the efficiency of the interviews, saving you and the SMEs time.

Building an effective Strawman involves four steps:

1. Build the shell for the content.

2. Collect preliminary content.

3. Populate the Strawman with content.

4. Identify gaps in content.

Step 2: Collect Information (via Interviewing)

Your Strawman has been populated, and you're finally ready to begin interviewing SMEs. Before you head out on your interviews, let's review the key Golden Rule (or principle) for conducting interviews:

Do it once!

Doing it right the first time eliminates re-work and inefficiencies. Data collection via interviews is the key event which can create re-work. If you do not structure and conduct an interview to ensure completeness of data collection, you may need to re-interview the SME. This creates inefficiencies and may also result in a negative impression of the interviewer!

To ensure that the interview process is complete and data has been captured accurately, work under the assumption that you have only one opportunity to collect the information from the SME.

Taping interviews increases inefficiencies as the tape will need to be transcribed.

How can you ensure that you will collect all required data from the SME in one interview? You're actually already almost halfway to accomplishing this goal because you've already populated the Strawman with preliminary content.

The approach we use for conducting complete interviews is:

- Develop an Interview Guide.
- Record complete notes (using the Interviewing Process outlined in Chapter 1).
- Debrief after the interview.

Before we discuss our interview approach further, we'll briefly cover the importance of note taking.

Note Taking During Interviews

Effective note taking during the interview process is critical for ensuring that you've collected complete and accurate data. The importance of effective note taking during the interview process cannot be overstated. What is effective note taking?

- Note taking should appear seamless to the SME (i.e., they should not be waiting for you to complete your notes).

- The notes should be complete and accurate, following the "do it once" rule.

- Your peers should be able to understand the notes.

To accomplish all of this, you'll need a structured proven methodology for note taking and some practice. The methodology must:

- Be easy and efficient.

- Be structured to ensure that you ask necessary follow-up questions during the interview (versus later).

- Generate legible and intelligible notes.

Select your note taking method prior to the interview, based on the type of interview. If you are collecting detailed procedural information, we recommend a flowcharting methodology. If the interview is less procedural in nature (i.e., you are collecting content for the narrative sections of the manual), we recommend adopting one of the proven note taking methodologies.

Flowcharting

While there are numerous flowcharting methodologies, we have found data flow diagramming to work very well for SME interviews. Data flow diagrams (DFDs) were invented by Larry Constantine, the developer of structured design for developing systems applications.

We like data flow diagramming for its simplicity, speed and usefulness in generating follow-up questions. The methodology utilizes only four symbols:

- A rectangle to indicate a person/group/organization outside of the flow (external entity).

- A circle or bubble to represent an activity or process.

- Two parallel lines to indicate a file or data store.

- A line connecting two of the other symbols to represent the flow of data to/from an activity, file or external entity.

We use the methodology fairly flexibly. If data is flowing to or from a system, we generally add a symbol to represent the system.

With a little practice, anyone can use data flow diagramming to draw a "picture" of a process or procedure. Freehand drawing works really well; the lines do not need to be straight. With data flow diagramming, a lot of data can be incorporated into one page – "a picture is worth more than a thousand words." Most people really like pictures, because pictures engage additional senses (vision and touch). Frequently, interviewees will add to or modify the picture. If you are interviewing an SME who races through their description of a process, showing them a picture of the process and getting them involved in drawing it tend to be helpful in slowing them down.

What we particularly like about the data flow diagram methodology is its ability to surface follow-up questions.

Let's look at a sample DFD that describes the following process:

- The Customer places an order for some goods with the Company.

- The Company verifies their credit card information (1).

- The order is processed and the items are shipped (2), and the Customer is sent an email confirmation.

- The Customer's account is updated with the transaction (3), and the Customer is advised of updated account information.

- The Customer may advise the Company of the need to change account information.

Sample Data Flow Diagram:

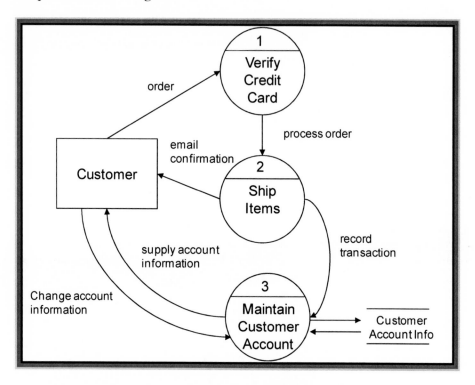

The flow leads to numerous follow-up questions, such as:

- How was the order placed? Telephone, Internet, in person?

- The Customer places the order, and the first process is Verify Credit Card. The next bubble, Ship Items, assumes that the credit card was approved. What happens if the credit card is not verified?

- How was the order processed?

- How does the Customer advise the Company of changes needed to their account information?

- How does the Company supply account information to the Customer?

You can find more detail on data flow diagrams in Wikipedia or by searching for "data flow diagrams" on the Internet.

We highly recommend using some sort of "picture" methodology, especially for collecting detailed process or procedure related information. Choose an approach that works for you; it will dramatically improve your note taking speed, accuracy and completeness.

Note Taking Systems

If the data you are collecting is less procedural in character, we recommend adopting one or a combination of note taking systems, such as the Cornell Method utilized typically by college students. Search for the term "Note taking" on the Web for more information on various systems. Experiment with what works best for you. Remember, your note taking system should:

- Be easy and efficient.
- Be structured to ensure that you ask necessary follow-up questions during the interview (versus later).
- Generate legible and intelligible notes.

Practice the methodology sufficiently before you begin interviewing SMEs. If you can't interview a friend for practice, then practice by watching TV shows and taking notes. While you obviously can't ask questions in this case, you can note your follow-up questions. Instructional types of TV shows, such as cooking or home fix-it shows, are good candidates for practice exercises. When you debrief, verify that your note taking system easily surfaced appropriate follow-up questions.

Since you will in most cases be collecting large amounts of data, we cannot overstate the importance of having rapid note taking systems in place prior to the interviewing process. Walking into interviews without a system in place for rapid note taking will seriously jeopardize the efficiency of the interview and your effectiveness as an interviewer. With many SMEs, you will not get a second chance to get them to commit their time to you.

Conducting Effective Interviews

In developing the draft Process Organizer, we covered many of the basics of the interview process. We think of interviewing as a process rather than an event because it's simply a data collection method with inputs, value-add steps and outputs. The inputs are the preparatory steps leading to the Strawman and the Interview Guide; the value-add step is the data collection (during the interview); and the output is the data. Let's take a minute to review the basics.

Conducting effective interviews is a skill that improves with practice and experience. We highly recommend debriefing after each interview and recording what went well and what did not. Record what you would do differently the next time. What this requires is being attentive not just to the collection of data but also to your interviewing approach during each interview. Being attentive to your interviewing approach and reflecting immediately after each interview will accelerate the development of your interviewing skills. Consider also observing professional interviewers on TV. Select an interviewer you admire and analyze what makes them effective.

Be over prepared for the interview. You should:

- Have a copy of the Strawman in case it makes sense to show it to the SME.

- Have developed an Interview Guide (more on this below).

- Know who the SME is (title, history, style (if possible)).

- Have your interviewing "tools" ready. Our recommendations:

    - Project sponsor memo/email introducing the project

    - A leather portfolio or professional notebook

    - Two automatic pencils and an eraser (preferably Pentel ClicEraser)

Schedule the meeting at a time convenient for the SME.

- Keep the meeting to no more than one hour. Longer meetings tend to become less productive. It's also easier for the SME to reserve 45 minutes to an hour versus multiple hours.

- Schedule the meeting away from the SME's workstation/office, if possible, to minimize distractions and interruptions.

- Always be on time for meetings, even if the culture of the organization does not encourage being on time.

As the interviewer, you control the interview. Controlling the interview yields efficiencies and builds your reputation as an effective interviewer. Controlling the interview is easy if:

- You've done all the recommended preparatory work (the Strawman, the Interview Guide and research on the SME).

- You appear well organized.

- You follow the recommended Interviewing Process.

The Interview Guide

The Interview Guide provides a structure for the interview and includes a list of all the questions you'll be asking the SME. You use the Interview Guide before the meeting as a planning tool and during the meeting to guide the meeting and ensure that everything has been covered. The Interview Guide generally includes the following:

1. Introduction

   - Thank the interviewee for their time; confirm time allowance

   - Introduce self and department (or organization)

   - Give overview of project (show sponsor email/memo)

   - Give overview of data collection process

   - Introduce Process Organizer

   - Explain purpose of meeting

2. Questions

   - List questions for general interview

   - Use Strawman for procedural questions

3. Closure

- Schedule another meeting if unable to cover all questions
- Summarize next steps (action items) with time frames
  - Deliverables from SME
  - Deliverables from interviewer
- Thank SME for time

You can either type up the Interview Guide (which is helpful for re-use for other interviews) or handwrite it. What's important is that you have planned the interview in advance and are now prepared to conduct an efficient interview.

The Soft Side of Conducting Interviews

Up to this point we have focused primarily on the technical (or hard) side of conducting efficient interviews. When interviewing SMEs, it's important to also be attentive to the human (or soft) side of conducting interviews. The interviewee's style, attitude and feelings about the interview may impact the success of the interview. For those of us blessed with a high emotional IQ, managing the human side of an interview may be less of a challenge. For most of us less blessed, the following strategies are helpful. We have developed these strategies over many years of interviewing SMEs, and these have worked for us (in most cases!).

Being respectful and appreciative of the SME's time

We've already touched on the importance of scheduling the meeting at the SME's convenience. We reinforce our respect for their time in several ways:

- Always, always be on time. If the meeting is in a conference room, be early and have all your materials set up to maximize efficiency. If you are meeting in their office, be right on time – not early or late.

- When reviewing the purpose of the project, we highlight the WIIFM ("what's in it for me"), focusing on how the manual will make the SME's life easier and reduce the amount of time they will need to spend providing subject matter information. For example, the manual might be a tool for facilitating training, a resource for auditors or systems developers, etc.

- When describing how the interview will be conducted, we indicate that the approach is designed to minimize the amount of time they will need to spend with us. We then briefly explain the Strawman technique.

- We act in ways that demonstrate our respect for their time. We show up to the interview thoroughly prepared and able to keep the interview moving along efficiently. We deliver drafts on schedule.

<u>Building rapport</u>

Rapport building should begin during the first few minutes of the meeting. If you know the SME, it should be fairly easy to build rapport during these introductory minutes by chatting about a common interest.

If you don't know the SME, rapport building is critical. Take cues from the SME as you introduce yourself, and model your style accordingly. If the SME seems impatient to begin, it's best to begin the interview quickly and keep the pace fairly fast. If the SME seems anxious, you might break the ice by referring to something discovered about the SME during backgrounding which can be safely raised. For example, you might say, "I understand that you have been working in Accounts Payable for over eight years." If, on the other hand, the SME appears relaxed and friendly, they will tend to break the ice!

<u>Being attentive</u>

Being attentive to the SME signals that you value the information they are providing and their expertise. The importance of attending to the SME cannot be overemphasized. We have interviewed all types of SMEs – at all levels of an organization; at various levels of education; with a variety of capabilities, experience sets, abilities to communicate, and interest in providing us with good data. We have found that most people will share their expertise with someone who actively shows that the expertise is highly valued.

You can demonstrate attention in several ways:

- Look at the SME at all times, unless you are taking notes.

- Avoid distractions.

- Ensure that facial expressions and body language convey interest.

- Verbally signal the SME that the information they are providing is important and helpful to the project. For example:

  - Occasionally, make a comment about the data. While a non-evaluative comment often works best (e.g., "that's interesting"), sometimes a somewhat-evaluative comment is appropriate (e.g., "that's really complex" or "this is really time sensitive").

  - Comments that are complimentary to the SME can also work well. For example, the "that's really complex" comment mentioned above is also complimentary.

  - Ask follow-up questions.

There are many articles and books that provide more information and valuable guidance on managing the soft side of the interview process. Also, we highly recommend that you watch interviews conducted by news reporters on TV and focus on how the interviewer manages the interview.

The Interviewing Process

Moving back to the technical side of the interview, let's review the Interviewing Process introduced in Chapter 1.

1. Introduce purpose of meeting
2. Ask questions
3. Confirm understanding
4. Modify your notes
5. Confirm completeness
6. Review next steps

After the ice is broken, introduce the purpose of the project and the meeting. Confirm the time allotment for the meeting to avoid surprise departures.

Begin with the first question or logical series of questions, taking notes based on the SME's responses. Summarize the SME's response to confirm your understanding and the correctness of your notes. If you are flowcharting the process, you might want to show the flow diagram to the SME. Make any necessary corrections to your notes or flowchart.

At the end of the interview, ensure completeness by summarizing the data you have collected. You and/or the SME may have missed critical data.

Now, going back to our Accounts Payable example, let's take a look at an interview with an SME on the Vendor Maintenance process. You have already developed some questions, which you added to the Strawman procedure. You included questions about inputs, value adds and outputs.

Sample Procedure with Preliminary Content:

3.1	Vendor Maintenance
3.1.1	Set up New Vendor

Responsibility:
Involved Parties:
System(s):
Procedures:

- How is information about new vendors received by AP? (Input)
  - Memo; email

- What information does AP need to set up a new vendor? (Input)

- Is there an approval process for new vendors? (Value add)

- How do they capture new vendor static data on their system? (Value add)

- Does anyone need to be advised of the setup? (Output)

- Must any documents be filed? (Output)

The next step is to prepare an Interview Guide for the meeting:

Sample Interview Guide:

Interviewee: Jane Brown, SME Accounts Payable
Topic: Vendor Maintenance, Set up New Vendor
Time: 6/8 10 am – 11 am
Place: Conference Room C

Documents Required:
Sponsor email
Process Organizer
Strawman for Set up New Vendor
Interview Guide

Introduction:
Thank for time; confirm time allowance of 1 hour
Introduce self and department (or organization)
Overview of project (show sponsor email/memo)
Overview of data collection process
    •   Strawman
    •   Today's interview
    •   Verification
    •   Modification
    •   Approval
Introduce Process Organizer
Purpose of meeting – focus on setup of new vendors

Questions:
What system does Accounts Payable utilize?
Can you describe the process for setting up new vendors on the system?
Ask Strawman questions if SME does not cover

Closure:
Schedule another meeting if unable to cover all questions
Summarize next steps (action items) with time frames
On _____, I'll return to observe the setup of a new vendor
By _____, I'll email you a draft of the procedure
Thank SME for time

You may have noticed that the questions on the Interview Guide are different from the questions included on the Strawman procedure. We find that it is beneficial to ask high-level questions first. In this example the high-level question is:

"Can you describe the process for setting up new vendors on the system?"

If we begin with very specific questions, we may influence the SME to provide narrow answers and miss important data. We have found it's best to apply Golden Rule 2 – "Always, always work from the top down" – and begin with a high-level question. The SME's response to the high-level question will probably provide answers to each of our Strawman questions. In case the response does not cover our Strawman questions, we can then raise those questions (e.g., "Must any documents be filed?").

With this in mind, let's now walk through an example of a data collection interview.

Begin the interview process by introducing yourself with a handshake, if appropriate. Thank the interviewee for their time. Review the purpose of the project, showing them the project sponsor's email. Mention how the manual will be used, along with potential benefits to the SME (e.g., training of new staff, reduced need for SME to explain process). Confirm that the interview should take no more than one hour.

Introduce the draft Process Organizer, describing its purpose, and then focus on the Vendor Maintenance process. Confirm that Vendor Maintenance includes:

- Set up New Vendor
- Modify Vendor Information
- Close Vendor Account

The SME may indicate that there is a vendor screening process, which they ensure is conducted on an annual basis. You add a new section to the Process Organizer: 3.1.4 Ensure Vendors Screened.

Ask the SME what system is utilized by Accounts Payable. The SME says that Accounts Payable uses Peachtree.

Ask the SME to describe the process for setting up new vendors, beginning with how they are notified about a new vendor. Since this type of process lends itself to flowcharting, flowchart the process described by the SME.

The SME indicates that an email is received from Corporate Sourcing instructing them to set up the vendor. They call the vendor contact to obtain additional information, including the tax ID of the vendor and payment instructions. They advise the contact of their preference to receive invoices electronically, via PDF. They fax a form to the vendor for completion. When the form is returned with the information, they set up the vendor on the Peachtree system.

While the SME describes the process, you draw the following flow:

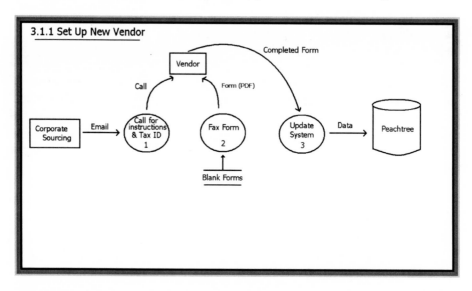

You show the flow to the SME, and the SME suggests that the line from bubble 3 to the Peachtree system be labeled "Vendor Data" instead of "Data." She also indicates that after the system is updated the information is verified.

You ask the SME:

- Who receives the email instruction?

- Who updates the system?

- Who verifies the data?

The SME indicates that the Static Data Associate performs all the steps. The verification is a sight verification, not a keystroke verification. After the data is sight verified, it is released into Peachtree.

You update the flow as follows and review it with the SME:

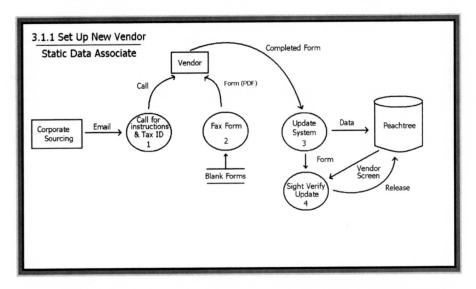

Checking the flow, you notice that the flow does not indicate what happens to the email instruction from Corporate Sourcing and the completed form from the vendor. When asked, the SME indicates that the documents are filed in a file set up for the vendor.

You update the flow as follows:

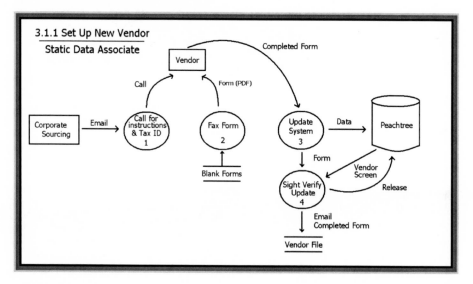

Show the flow to the SME, reviewing each activity, and confirm that the flow is complete.

Ask the SME for copies of:

- A sample email instruction from Corporate Sourcing
- A copy of the form which is faxed to the Vendor

Ask the SME for a contact name for obtaining screenshots of the input step.

Thank the SME for their time and summarize (and note) next steps:

- The SME will provide copies of an email instruction and the faxed form.
- You will contact a Static Data Associate to observe the input process and obtain screenshots.
- You will write up the procedure for the SME to verify.

If possible, include time frames in your summary of next steps.

File the notes from the interview in the Project Workbook.

Interviews Involving Multiple SMEs

Implied in the Interviewing Process described is that you are interviewing one person. Will the same process work with interviews with several SMEs?

For interviews with multiple SMEs to collect procedural data, we recommend using an easel chart or board for flowcharting so that all participants can easily view the flowchart. The easel chart is preferred, as the easel paper can easily be transported. You may want to use colored markers. Just make sure that the interview room is equipped with all the equipment and supplies that you need ahead of time.

For interviews with multiple SMEs to collect narrative content, you should be fine recording data on a notepad. The challenge in interviewing multiple SMEs is generally to ensure that everyone is involved in the interview process and is in agreement. Summarizing and asking for everyone's confirmation (step 3 of the Interviewing Process) is critical.

Group dynamics can sometimes be a challenge. While typically one of the interviewees will take the lead in responding to questions and may try to control the interview, you can manage this if you consistently apply step 3 of the Interviewing Process. More problematic to manage is when the SMEs disagree. If there is disagreement, try to isolate the specifics and record each view; then, table the issue until you can get independent confirmation outside of the meeting. The goal is not to get bogged down in the meeting.

Sample Interview with Multiple SMEs:

Speaker	Conversation
You	*Describe the process for setting up new vendors.*
SME 1	*We receive an email from Sourcing, instructing us to set up the new vendor. We call the contact on the email to obtain their tax ID number and their payment instructions.*
SME 2	*We don't call the contact – the information is on the email from Sourcing.*
SME 1	*I've never seen that information on the email.*
SME 2	*Yes, Corporate Sourcing should supply that information – and if it's missing or incomplete we send it back to Sourcing who gets the information.*
You	*We can confirm Corporate Sourcing's understanding of their responsibility separately. Let's keep moving. What happens after you have all the information needed about the Vendor?*

When there are disagreements, your strategy should always be:

- Don't get bogged down.
- Don't make anyone wrong.
- Control the interview.

We frequently find inconsistencies in organizations, especially those without standard operating procedures. Your project is a good opportunity to surface those inconsistencies and to work with the SMEs to develop an optimal process. If you cannot later on get a resolution on how the process should work, refer the issue to the project sponsor.

Phone Interviews

We are conducting interviews more frequently via phone. Phone interviews can work if you are not collecting a lot of data and/or you have a strong Strawman. You'll have a strong Strawman if you have already developed a manual for the organization in one location (e.g., Accounts Payable in Chicago) and are now completing a manual for a similar group in another location (e.g., Accounts Payable in London).

We generally email the Strawman procedure(s) to the SME for review prior to the phone interview. Then, we can focus on differences. In some cases, the SME will note differences on the document using a change-tracking feature in their word-processing program.

We have conducted phone interviews with multiple SMEs when we don't have any type of Strawman. This type of interview can be difficult to manage, especially when the SMEs disagree, because there are no visual clues. In these cases, it's probably best to get on a plane!

Interviews with Related Departments

Depending on the type of manual you are developing, you may need to meet with representatives of related departments. These departments may interface with the subject group of your manual, or, for compliance related manuals, may be policy setting groups. Interface departments are discussed in "Confirming Data with Interfacing Departments" on page 78.

If you are developing a compliance related manual, you should reference policies and regulations. To begin the collection process:

1. First, ask the project sponsor which policies and regulations apply to the group. The project sponsor will generally be able to provide you with a partial list.

2. Develop a list of policy setting groups in your organization. Present the list to the project sponsor or SME, and ask which of these groups' policies might apply. Ask the project sponsor whether they can provide the name of a contact in the policy setting group.

3. Contact each policy setting group, explaining the purpose of the project and referencing the project introduction email that they

should have received. If the project sponsor or SME has given you a list of Strawman policies and regulations, forward the applicable policies and regulations on to the policy setting group for review.

4. Build a policy and regulation matrix, and begin populating the matrix as you collect the applicable policies and regulations. Depending on the number and type of policies, we recommend separating the list into categories, such as Global vs. Local policies, or Business vs. Personnel vs. Operational related policies (see Appendix 2: Policy/Regulation Matrix Shell).

5. The completed matrix will need to be verified with the project sponsor or SME (see "Step 4: Verify Content" on page 77).

Now you're ready to begin drafting the procedure!

Recap:

To collect information via interviews, you'll need to be able to record large amounts of data quickly and accurately. Adopting efficient note taking and flowcharting methodologies is critical for success.

Preparation is 90% of success!

Before you step into the interview you should have a robust:

- Set of Strawman procedures
- Interview Guide

Follow the same Interviewing Process you used to collect data for the Process Organizer:

1. Introduce purpose of meeting
2. Ask questions
3. Confirm understanding
4. Modify your notes
5. Confirm completeness
6. Review next steps

Step 3: Draft Content

We recommend drafting content right after the interview is completed. You will probably find it easier to write the content while the material is still fresh in your mind. You'll also be able to get the content back to the SME fairly quickly for verification.

We use a two-step process. We draft the content first; we scrub, or edit, the content later. Our rule of thumb is to just get something rough on paper. The content can be tightened up and wordsmithed later. Our rules for writing the narrative sections and procedures sections are outlined below.

Drafting Narrative Sections

Our rules for structuring narrative content are identical for all manuals, regardless of the audience. We assume that the manual will be read by individuals with different purposes. Some readers will be interested in an overview, others will be interested in some detail and still others will be interested in a lot of detail.

An individual looking for an overview might only look at the table of contents or skim the introductory sections. We consider this in designing the introductory sections of the manual. Since the procedures are already organized via processes, the list of procedures titles provides a good overview of the group's activities.

To promote effective skimming within the introductory sections, we follow a few important organizational rules.

- Organize the paragraphs within a section so that each focuses on a key point/idea.

- Summarize that key point/idea in the first sentence (the title sentence).

- Use the remainder of the paragraph to expand upon and/or support the title sentence.

This type of structure allows the skimmer to pick up the essence of the content by reading just the title sentence of each paragraph of the section.

For an example of this approach, take a look at how this section is structured. Here are the title of the section and the title sentence of each paragraph:

Drafting Narrative Sections

Our rules for structuring narrative content are identical for all manuals, regardless of the audience.

An individual looking for an overview might only look at the table of contents or skim the introductory sections.

To promote effective skimming within the introductory sections, we follow a few important organizational rules.

For an example of this approach, take a look at how this section is structured.

As you can see, the structure of the paragraphs in a section and the title sentences work together to facilitate skimming. You can easily test the structure of your content by conducting a similar exercise.

Strategic Considerations

Our view is that organizations develop manuals for strategic reasons, such as:

- Training
- Coordination
- New function/business/system
- Risk management
- Regulatory requirement
- Marketing

If there is not a clear strategic reason for spending time and money to develop a manual, then the manual should probably not be written and you should not be wasting your time on it.

Understanding the strategic purpose of the manual is important, because it enables you to design the manual to meet the needs of the target audience and to determine the appropriate theme or message for the manual. Let's take a look at some examples.

Training is a fairly common strategy. A function may be performed by numerous staff, and expansion and/or turnover are anticipated. A merger may have occurred, and staff within one of the organizations requires training on systems and processes. Manuals intended for training purposes must be instructional. They usually:

- are written at a granular level and include graphics and examples

- use a straightforward style so that they are easy for the target audience to read and understand

- are organized to expedite finding instructions

- present easy-to-follow instructions

The manual's underlying theme or message should convince the target audience that they will be successful in following the instructions, a theme which is similar to the theme of this book!

Let's take a look at another example – a manual which is a regulatory or audit requirement. The group or function may be required by internal audit or regulators to document their procedures. Auditors and regulators usually care about the adequacy of controls. This type of manual should therefore focus on control points and should:

- be written at a less detailed level and may include flowcharts

- be oriented stylistically (language, sentence length and structure) to auditors (for guidance, review an audit report)

- focus on risks and how they are controlled

- include a section on roles and responsibilities with job descriptions

- reference regulations and the firm's policies
- include samples of control reports

The manual's underlying theme or message should convince the target audience that the group understands its risk environment and, in response, has effective controls in place.

Drafting Procedures

While the narrative sections of the manual present an overview of the process, including risks and controls, the procedures describe specifically how the process is completed. The **key rules** for drafting procedures are as follows:

1. A procedure should begin with an input, which is transformed via a process into an output (or outputs).

   input→ process→ output

2. Procedural steps should be brief and indicate who performs the step, what action is being performed (value add) and the result.

   who→ action→ result

3. Background information is not included in the procedural step. If context is important, provide the context in narrative format before the procedural steps or, for brief contextual information, within parentheses in the procedural step.

4. To simplify maintenance, policies and rules are not described in the procedural steps but are referenced into the procedure. For example:

   The Static Data Associate obtains the Tax Identification Number (TIN) from the vendor in compliance with the Vendor Tax Reporting Policy.

   rather than

   The Vendor Tax Reporting Policy requires that a TIN is obtained from each vendor. The Static Data Associate verifies that a TIN has been obtained from the vendor.

Let's take a look at a sample draft procedure based on the flowchart for Set up New Vendor from our interview with the Accounts Payable SME.

Flowchart for Set up New Vendor:

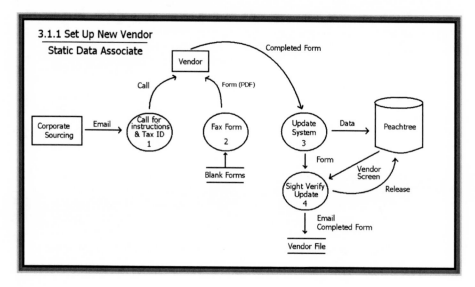

Sample Draft Procedure for Set up New Vendor:

3.1   Vendor Maintenance

3.1.1   Set up New Vendor

Responsibility: Static Data Associate (SDA)
Involved Parties: Corporate Sourcing
System(s):   Peachtree
Procedures:

1. Static Data Associate receives an email instruction (Exhibit 3.1.1a) from Corporate Sourcing to set up a new vendor and reviews email for completeness following up with Corporate Sourcing if necessary.
2. Call vendor contact for additional information and indicate information provided on email from Corporate Sourcing including:
   - Tax identification number
   - Payment instructions
   - Ability to send invoice via PDF
   - Fax number
3. Complete fax cover sheet and fax form (Exhibit 3.1.1b) to new vendor.
4. When vendor faxes completed form, SDA checks form for completeness and follows up with vendor contact if necessary.
5. SDA accesses Maintain Vendors screen on Peachtree (Exhibit 3.1.1c) and enters required data from email and New Vendor Form.
6. SDA sight checks the screen to verify that information has been entered accurately and completely.
7. SDA completes any necessary changes and releases the update in Peachtree.
8. SDA sets up a file for the new vendor and files paperwork in folder including:
   - Email from Corporate Sourcing
   - Completed fax form
9. File new vendor folder in Vendor File.

Link(s):

Let's compare this procedure to the rules.

<u>Rule 1:</u> Is there an input, process and output for the overall procedure?

The input is the email from Sourcing. The output (or result) is the vendor information captured on Peachtree (somewhat implicit) and the vendor file (explicit). In many procedures, the output will be implicit (i.e., embedded in the procedure or not obviously stated).

<u>Rule 2:</u> Are procedural steps brief and inclusive of who performs the step, what action is being performed and the result?

In cases where the same individual performs all steps, it is not necessary to repeat this information in each step. Steps 2 and 3 in this example do not specify that the SDA is performing the steps.

Although the action being performed in each step is clear, in some cases the result is implicit. For example, for step 3 of the procedure – "Complete fax cover sheet and fax form (Exhibit 3.1.1b) to new vendor." – the result is that the vendor has received the form for completion.

<u>Rule 3:</u> Is background information segregated from the procedural step?

In our example, there is no background information. Let's add some, though, so that you can see how it would be handled. Let's introduce an approval process prior to Accounts Payable being advised of a new vendor.

Sample Draft Procedure with Background Information:

3.1   Vendor Maintenance

3.1.1   Set up New Vendor

Responsibility: Static Data Associate (SDA)
Involved Parties: Corporate Sourcing
System(s):   Peachtree
Procedures:

Corporate Sourcing is responsible for approving new vendors. After a new vendor is approved, they advise Accounts Payable of approval and payment terms.

1. Static Data Associate receives an email instruction (Exhibit 3.1.1a) from Corporate Sourcing to set up a new vendor and reviews email for completeness following up with Corporate Sourcing if necessary.
2. Call vendor contact for additional information and indicate information provided on email from Corporate Sourcing including:
   - Tax identification number
   - Payment instructions
   - Ability to send invoice via PDF
   - Fax number
3. Complete fax cover sheet and fax form (Exhibit 3.1.1b) to new vendor.
4. When vendor faxes completed form, SDA checks form for completeness and follows up with vendor contact if necessary.
5. SDA accesses Maintain Vendors screen on Peachtree (Exhibit 3.1.1c) and enters required data from email and New Vendor Form.
6. SDA sight checks the screen to verify that information has been entered accurately and completely.
7. SDA completes any necessary changes and releases the update in Peachtree.
8. SDA sets up a file for the new vendor and files paperwork in folder including:
   - Email from Corporate Sourcing
   - Completed fax form
9. File new vendor folder in Vendor File.

Link(s):

<u>Rule 4:</u> Are policies and rules segregated from procedures?

In our example, we have not included any information about policies or rules. Let's take a look at how we would reference a policy or rule in the Set up New Vendor procedure. Depending on the requirement, text can be added to the background narrative preceding the procedure (bolded in the following example) or in the procedural step. The actual policy can then be linked into the procedure and added as an appendix.

Sample Draft Procedure with Reference to a Policy:

3.1   Vendor Maintenance

3.1.1   Set up New Vendor

Responsibility: Static Data Associate (SDA)
Involved Parties: Corporate Sourcing
System(s):   Peachtree
Procedures:

Corporate Sourcing is responsible for approving new vendors. After a new vendor is approved, they advise Accounts Payable of approval and payment terms. **Accounts Payable is required to obtain a Tax Identification Number from all vendors.**

1. Static Data Associate receives an email instruction (Exhibit 3.1.1a) from Corporate Sourcing to set up a new vendor and reviews email for completeness following up with Corporate Sourcing if necessary.
2. Call vendor contact for additional information and indicate information provided on email from Corporate Sourcing including:
   - Tax identification number (**per Vendor Tax Reporting Policy**)
   - Payment instructions
   - Ability to send invoice via PDF
   - Fax number
3. Complete fax cover sheet and form (Exhibit 3.1.1b) and fax to new vendor.
4. When vendor faxes completed form, SDA checks form for completeness and follows up with vendor contact if necessary.
5. SDA accesses Maintain Vendors screen on Peachtree (Exhibit 3.1.1c) and enters required data from email and New Vendor Form.
6. SDA sight checks the screen to verify that information has been entered accurately and completely.
7. SDA completes any necessary changes and releases the update in Peachtree.
8. SDA sets up a file for the new vendor and files paperwork in folder including:
   - Email from Corporate Sourcing
   - Completed fax form
9. File new vendor folder in Vendor File.

Link(s):
Vendor Tax Reporting Policy – www.ABCcorp.com/Policies/vendortaxpolicy.htm

---

Appendix 3: Procedure Writing Tips contains additional information on drafting procedural content.

Missing Data

You may have noticed that we added additional content that was not on the flow to the draft procedure. Missing from the flow is any reference to following up with either Corporate Sourcing (step 1) or the vendor (step 4). There is also no mention of writing any information on the email (step 2). While the interviewer missed obtaining this information during the interview, the blanks have been filled in with reasonable possibilities (placeholders) on the draft procedure. This will facilitate the review with the SME. While the goal is to obtain all the information in the interview, if you do miss an aspect of the process, simply create a placeholder for verification with the SME.

Flowchart for Set up New Vendor:

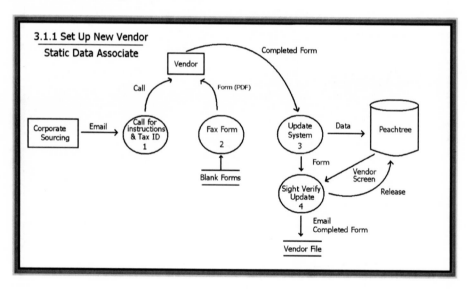

Sample Draft Procedure with Placeholder Text:

3.1   Vendor Maintenance

3.1.1   Set up New Vendor

Responsibility: Static Data Associate (SDA)
Involved Parties: Corporate Sourcing
System(s):   Peachtree
Procedures:

Corporate Sourcing is responsible for approving new vendors. After a new vendor is approved, they advise Accounts Payable of approval and payment terms. Accounts Payable is required to obtain a Tax Identification Number from all vendors.

1. Static Data Associate receives an email instruction (Exhibit 3.1.1a) from Corporate Sourcing to set up a new vendor and reviews email for completeness following up with Corporate Sourcing if necessary.
2. Call vendor contact for additional information and indicate information provided on email from Corporate Sourcing including:
    - Tax identification number (per Vendor Tax Reporting Policy)
    - Payment instructions
    - Ability to send invoice via PDF
    - Fax number
3. Complete fax cover sheet and form (Exhibit 3.1.1b) and fax to new vendor.
4. When vendor faxes completed form, SDA checks form for completeness and follows up with vendor contact if necessary.
5. SDA accesses Maintain Vendors screen on Peachtree (Exhibit 3.1.1c) and enters required data from email and New Vendor Form.
6. SDA sight checks the screen to verify that information has been entered accurately and completely.
7. SDA completes any necessary changes and releases the update in Peachtree.
8. SDA sets up a file for the new vendor and files paperwork in folder including:
    - Email from Corporate Sourcing
    - Completed fax form
9. File new vendor folder in Vendor File.

Link(s):
Vendor Tax Reporting Policy – www.ABCcorp.com/Policies/vendortaxpolicy.htm

---

Now you're ready to begin verifying the content!

Recap:

The strategic purpose of the manual drives the design of the manual, its content and underlying theme or message. Before you draft content, learn as much as possible about the intended audience for the manual and how they will use the manual.

The narrative sections of the manual should be structured for multiple audiences: those looking for an overview as well as those looking for more detail.

The key rules for drafting procedures:

1. Follow this structure for the overall procedure:

    input→ process→ output

2. Follow this structure for procedural steps:

    who→ action→ result

3. Keep it simple by limiting background information.

4. Keep it easy to maintain by omitting descriptions of policies and rules from procedural steps.

Step 4: Verify Content

If you are developing an operations manual or a training manual, you will most likely need to conduct observations. For compliance related manuals, you may need to conduct observations for specific, more granular procedures.

Our practice is to conduct observations after the procedure is written. The observations serve to confirm the procedure and to provide added detail where needed. This practice is consistent with our first and second Golden Rules – "Never, never start from scratch" and "Always, always work from the top down." The draft of the more detailed procedure will then be verified with the SME.

Conducting Observations

Depending on the process, it may make sense to conduct observations. Missing data and/or more detailed data can be obtained during the observations. It's best to draft the procedure based on the SME interview first. This will surface missing data beforehand, so the observation can be used to collect the missing data.

A few notes on observations:

- It's generally optimal to observe when the individual being observed is not overwhelmed with work. If things are too quiet, however, the volume may be insufficient for observing multiple instances of the process. The best time for observations is generally when there is some volume and the person being observed is not stressed and can answer questions.

- If you are observing a high volume process and timing is sensitive, you may only be able to observe the workflow and not ask many questions. In these situations, we generally try to be unobtrusive and wait until the workflow slows down to ask questions.

- Our rule of thumb for determining how many times to observe a process is to assess similarities across the number of observed instances of the process. If there is little variation, we stop the observation. If there is variation, we continue to make sure we have captured the reasons for the variation.

- In cases in which volumes are low, the SME being observed may walk us through the process with examples of paperwork and/or input screens. If the manual is for training purposes, we'll make sure we probe to ensure we have captured all the typical variations in the process.

- If more than one individual performs the process or part of the process which is being observed, the best person to observe is generally the individual with some experience. If you can, try to avoid those with little experience and those individuals who have been performing the activities for many years.

Depending on the activity, you may find that using your flowchart of the process makes more sense than using the procedure. You can take notes on the flowchart and show it to the individual you are observing if necessary.

Confirming Data with Interfacing Departments

For procedures which interface with other internal departments, we recommend contacting the interface to confirm the data. In our example, there is an interface with the Corporate Sourcing Department. The interviewer should obtain a contact name in Corporate Sourcing from the SME and arrange to confirm the information. If the information is extensive or critical, a meeting may be in order. Otherwise, either a phone call or an email including the procedure will suffice. We are not interested in Corporate Sourcing's entire process – only how they interface with Accounts Payable.

It's important to confirm interface interactions to ensure accuracy. Our experience is that interfaces are the points in a process where breakdowns tend to occur.

Sample Interview with an Interface:

I am developing a procedures manual for Accounts Payable.

I understand that Corporate Sourcing instructs Accounts Payable to set up new vendors on their system.

Can you describe how you do this?

If inconsistencies are uncovered in the process, follow-up will be required to determine what the process should be.

Verifying Data

Depending on the procedure and your agreement with the SME, verification can be via a meeting or email. If there are a number of open issues, it's best to meet with the SME briefly in person. We typically highlight the parts of the procedure we have questions on.

During the verification meeting, provide the SME with a copy of the draft procedure with any open issues highlighted. Indicate to the SME that the highlighted text represents areas for which you have some questions. You should be able to capture changes to the procedure on the procedure itself rather than a separate sheet of paper. If there are extensive changes to the procedure, you will want to examine your data collection process.

You're getting close to the finish line! You are almost ready for sign-off on the manual by the sponsor!

Recap:

For detailed procedures:

- Draft the procedure based on the interview with the SME.

- Conduct observations to confirm the procedure and collect further details.

- Verify the procedure with the SME.

For more general procedures:

- Draft the procedure based on the interview with the SME.

- For missing data, create placeholders in the procedure and highlight for discussion with the SME.

- Verify the procedure with the SME.

Any content collected from interface departments should also be verified with the interface department.

Step 5: Modify Content

As each part of the manual is verified, modifications are made to specific sections. Depending on the scope and sensitivity of the modification, a re-verification with the SME may be needed. Make sure that you have a record of who signed off and when, either on the draft-copy section of the manual or on copies of any emails from the SME indicating that they were OK with the content. These sign-offs should all be in your Project Workbook under the "Verified Sections" tab, so that you can easily retrieve them if needed.

When you have completed verifications with all the SMEs, you should review the entire manual and get the manual ready for sign-off by the sponsor and key stakeholders. The final review and "scrub" should identify any:

- Inconsistencies within the narrative and procedures, and inconsistencies between the narrative and the procedures sections
- Gaps in completeness
- Inconsistencies in the flow and voice of the text
- Editing issues, including:
  - Grammar errors
  - Spelling errors
  - Clarity issues
- Formatting issues

If your organization does not have a standard format for its manuals, please see Appendix 4: Formatting and Review Standards for our formatting standards.

Further checks will be performed during the packaging of the manual, which we will discuss in detail in Chapter 3 – Release Stage.

Exhibits, appendices and references are generally incorporated after the final sign-off. If flowcharts are required, these are also completed after the final sign-off to minimize re-work.

When you have completed all modifications and the final scrub of the manual, the draft manual is ready for sign-off. The manual should still be identified as a draft until the final changes have been received from the sponsor and made.

You're close to the finish line!

Recap:

Modifications to and sign-off on the content by the SMEs should be maintained in the Project Workbook for future reference.

After the SMEs have approved the various sections of the manual, and after a final scrub, the manual is ready to be reviewed by the sponsor.

In general, if the sponsor has any changes, they should be minor.

Step 6: Obtain Sign-off on Content

After we have made modifications to a manual and completed a final scrub, we generally email the manual to the project sponsor for review and arrange a review meeting. Emailing the manual prior to the meeting provides the sponsor with the opportunity to review the manual before the meeting.

The review meetings with the sponsor can vary significantly depending on the style and role of the sponsor. Be prepared to answer questions, and bring your Project Workbook with you to the meeting. Placing the clearly branded workbook (name of group and "Project Workbook" noted in large printed letters on the cover) on the table communicates to the sponsor that you've done your homework. If the sponsor does have questions, you should be able to retrieve the information quickly in your workbook.

Generally at this stage of the project, there should not be any major changes to the manual. We have developed hundreds of manuals, and we have found that by the time we get to this step issues have already been surfaced and remediated. If major changes are required, you'll need to determine why; although you may need to complete the manual first, be sure to invest time after the manual is published in analyzing what happened, so that you do not miss a learning opportunity.

After completing any necessary modifications, but before publishing the manual, email the sponsor that you are ready to publish the manual. Their reply or lack of reply constitutes their sign-off.

Congratulations – you are now ready to release the manual!

Recap:

When conducting the sign-off meeting with the sponsor, bring the Project Workbook, so that you are prepared to answer questions from the sponsor.

At this point in the process, any changes should be minor. If the sponsor has significant additions, changes or deletions to the manual, it's critical to understand why.

Chapter 3
Release Stage

Organizing a Manual Effectively

You've collected and verified all the data for your manual, and now you are looking forward to putting it all together and moving on to another priority. While it may be tempting to wrap the project up quickly, these last stages of the project are probably the most important.

How well the manual is organized will:

- determine its value as a resource to users and

- facilitate ongoing updates to the manual.

The value of your manual as an asset to your company and its employees depends on how well it is organized. Yes, accuracy of content is obviously important. If users cannot access the information they need quickly, however, they may question the usefulness of the manual.

The reliability of the manual's content also impacts the manual's credibility. Chances are that shortly after your manual is published, some of the content will be stale. The organization of the manual can either facilitate or hinder updates.

We recommend taking a hub-and-spoke approach to organizing a manual. We have found that this approach facilitates both accessibility and updates. The basic premise of the approach is to separate out the parts of the manual that change most often in order to facilitate updates. The hub is the core of the manual (the introductory narrative sections and the Procedures section).   The spokes are the supporting documents (i.e., the exhibits, appendices and references). Each supporting document is linked into the hub but is housed in its own section of the manual. The diagram below illustrates this approach.

The Hub-and-Spoke Approach to Organizing a Manual:

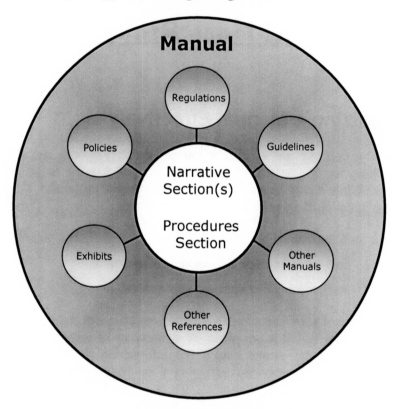

Generally, a manual will have four to five sections. In most cases, the hub comprises two or three main sections:

- Introduction
- Roles and Responsibilities (if a compliance related manual)
- Procedures

Usually there will be at least two to three sections of supporting reference material for operational and compliance related manuals.

- Exhibits

- Policies

- Other References

If the manual is to be published in hard copy, we recommend consolidating all of the references, with the exception of the exhibits, into an Appendices section.

So, a typical manual would include the following sections:

- Introduction

- Roles and Responsibilities (if a compliance related manual)

- Procedures

- Exhibits

- Appendices

Exhibits

Most procedural manuals include exhibits in procedures to provide greater detail or reference points. For example, in "Drafting Procedures" on page 67, we wrote a procedure for Set up New Vendor which included an exhibit of the email instruction Corporate Sourcing sent to Accounts Payable. This exhibit provides a reference point, a picture of the email, which is useful for the user of the manual. The exhibit also eliminates the need to detail in the Set up New Vendor procedure all of the information contained in the email. Should the information included in the email change at some point in the future, we could just include a new exhibit rather than update the procedure.

As you were developing content for the manual, you may have noted places where an exhibit made sense. At this point, go through the manual and finalize all the exhibits which add value. Resist adding exhibits which don't add value. There is a cost to adding exhibits, because any exhibits you add will need to be maintained.

Once you have finalized the draft list of exhibits, review and confirm the list with the SME(s). The SME(s) should be able to either provide copies (preferably electronic) of the exhibits or direct you to someone who can.

For each exhibit you collect, verify that the exhibit is readable. Electronic copies, particularly scanned documents, can sometimes be difficult to read. Also, depending on the manual, some exhibits may contain confidential information. In such cases, confirm that any confidential data has been redacted.

Each exhibit should be identified with a name and number. The name should help to identify the exhibit. For the email from Corporate Sourcing, for example, you might incorporate an identifier such as "Vendor Setup Email Instruction" in the exhibit name.

Each exhibit is numbered based on the section or procedure it supports. Each exhibit number includes a letter suffix, which helps to identify exhibits when multiple exhibits support a section or procedure (e.g., 3.4.2a for the first exhibit in 3.4.2; 3.4.2b for the second exhibit in 3.4.2). The numbers should be printed on the upper left corner of the exhibit to facilitate easy location by a reader of the manual.

It's easier to incorporate identifying names and numbers when the exhibits are in soft copy. If they are only available in hard copy, you will need to use a manual copy-and-paste process.

We recommend housing all exhibits in one section of the manual to keep the narrative and Procedures sections (the hub) tidier. The Exhibits section should contain a table of contents listing each exhibit and its number. Should the reader need more detail, they can access the Exhibits section. If there is a reason for placing an exhibit right behind the applicable section or procedure, though, then by all means place it there. Publishing a manual on a system for managing manuals that incorporates hyperlinks eliminates this issue.

Sample Exhibits Section Table of Contents:

4.0 – Exhibits

3.1.1a	Vendor Setup Email Instruction
3.1.1b	New Vendor Form
3.1.1c	Peachtree Maintain Vendors Screen

Appendices

Appendices may include a variety of reference material. Depending on the type of manual, we will sort appendices into categories if there are many appendices.

For compliance related manuals, we will generally organize the appendices into these categories:

- Policies

- Regulations

- Other References

Other References could include other manuals within the organization related to the subject manual, system user manuals, material from industry groups, brochures, and articles – essentially any reference material which may be of value to the reader of the manual.

For operational manuals, we may include policies and in some cases regulations or industry standards. Operational manuals can also benefit from referencing other manuals and guides, including system user manuals.

Each appendix should be clearly identified with its name. For references with multiple pages, we generally include the appendix name only on the first page.

If possible, for appendices we prefer to direct the reader to a Web address (on the Internet or your organization's intranet) rather than use a hard copy of the document. This facilitates maintenance. This approach assumes the Web address for the reference will not be modified.

As with the list of exhibits, it's best to review the list of appendices with the SME(s). Again, be selective with the appendices you include because there are implications for maintenance.

If the manual is to be published in hard copy format, we consolidate policies, regulations and other reference material into the Appendices section for ease of use and maintenance. The Appendices section should include a table of contents listing each appendix by name and number. We utilize numbered tabs to separate and identify appendices within the Appendices section; the tabs allow for easy access to appendices.

For example, if the Employee Code of Conduct Policy is Appendix 1, it would be listed in the Appendices table of contents as:

1. Employee Code of Conduct Policy

Behind Tab 1, users would find a hard copy of the policy, a reference to the owner of the policy or a website address.

If there are website addresses for all appendices in a manual, we will just include the website address in the table of contents, as shown below. This eliminates the need for tabs.

Sample Appendices Table of Contents with Website Addresses:

5.0 – Appendices

Accounts Payable - Summary of Applicable Policies	
Regulation / Policy	**Reference Notes**
Vendor Tax Reporting Policy	www.ABCcorp.com/Policies/vendortaxpolicy.htm
Employee Reimbursement Policy	www.ABCcorp.com/Policies/employeereimbursementpolicy.htm
Records Management Policy	www.ABCcorp.com/Policies/recordsmgmtpolicy.htm

Integrating Exhibits and Appendices into the Manual

If your manual is to be published on a system for managing policies and procedures (generally this would be a Web-based system), the system should facilitate change management. If your manual is to be published in hard copy – and perhaps stored electronically on a shared drive or document management system – you will find our approach to organizing and integrating the various parts of the manual helpful for change management.

Exhibits and appendices are separated out into distinct sections of the manual, as described above. Each exhibit or appendix is then linked into the manual hub. You should verify that each exhibit listed in the Exhibits section and each appendix listed in the Appendices section links into at least one main part of the manual.

We use different approaches for linking exhibits versus appendices into the main parts of the manual. For exhibits, we reference the exhibit by number directly in the text of the section or procedure it supports, as shown in the following example.

Sample Procedure with References to Exhibits:

3.1   Vendor Maintenance

3.1.1   Set up New Vendor

Responsibility: Static Data Associate (SDA)
Involved Parties: Corporate Sourcing
System(s):   Peachtree
Procedures:

Corporate Sourcing is responsible for approving new vendors. After a new vendor is approved, they advise Accounts Payable of approval and payment terms. Accounts Payable is required to obtain a Tax Identification Number from all vendors.

1. Static Data Associate receives an email instruction (Exhibit 3.1.1a) from Corporate Sourcing to set up a new vendor and reviews email for completeness following up with Corporate Sourcing if necessary.
2. Call vendor contact for additional information and indicate information provided on email from Corporate Sourcing including:
    - Tax identification number (per Vendor Tax Reporting Policy)
    - Payment instructions
    - Ability to send invoice via PDF
    - Fax number
3. Complete fax cover sheet and form (Exhibit 3.1.1b) and fax to new vendor.
4. When vendor faxes completed form, SDA checks form for completeness and follows up with vendor contact if necessary.
5. SDA accesses Maintain Vendors screen on Peachtree (Exhibit 3.1.1c) and enters required data from email and New Vendor Form.
6. SDA sight checks the screen to verify that information has been entered accurately and completely.
7. SDA completes any necessary changes and releases the update in Peachtree.
8. SDA sets up a file for the new vendor and files paperwork in folder including:
    - Email from Corporate Sourcing
    - Completed fax form
9. File new vendor folder in Vendor File.

Link(s):
Vendor Tax Reporting Policy – www.ABCcorp.com/Policies/vendortaxpolicy.htm

For appendices, we handle links to narrative introductory sections and procedures sections differently. In a narrative introductory section, we add a reference directly in the body of the text, as shown in the following example.

Sample Reference to a Policy in an Introductory Section:

1.9   Risk Control Processes

The Group has several policies and processes in place to ensure that prospective vendors are vetted appropriately. Corporate Sourcing coordinates the vetting process among various groups and is ultimately responsible for approving new vendors. For all approved vendors Accounts Payable obtains a tax identification number. Transactions are not processed for vendors without a tax identification number on file as per the *Vendor Tax Reporting Policy (www.ABCcorp.com/Policies/vendortaxpolicy.htm)*.

or

The Group has several policies and processes in place to ensure that prospective vendors are vetted appropriately. Corporate Sourcing coordinates the vetting process among various groups and is ultimately responsible for approving new vendors. For all approved vendors Accounts Payable obtains a tax identification number. Transactions are not processed for vendors without a tax identification number on file as per the *Vendor Tax Reporting Policy (Appendix 5)*.

In a procedure, we add a link to the appendix in a "Link(s)" box. Consolidating all appendix references at the bottom of the procedure is easier on the reader and the maintainer or owner of the manual.

Sample Reference to a Policy Using the Link(s) Box in a Procedure:

3.1   Vendor Maintenance

3.1.1   Set up New Vendor

Responsibility: Static Data Associate (SDA)
Involved Parties: Corporate Sourcing
System(s):   Peachtree
Procedures:

Corporate Sourcing is responsible for approving new vendors. After a new vendor is approved, they advise Accounts Payable of approval and payment terms. Accounts Payable is required to obtain a Tax Identification Number from all vendors.

1. Static Data Associate receives an email instruction (Exhibit 3.1.1a) from Corporate Sourcing to set up a new vendor and reviews email for completeness following up with Corporate Sourcing if necessary.
2. Call vendor contact for additional information and indicate information provided on email from Corporate Sourcing including:
   - Tax identification number (per Vendor Tax Reporting Policy)
   - Payment instructions
   - Ability to send invoice via PDF
   - Fax number
3. Complete fax cover sheet and form (Exhibit 3.1.1b) and fax to new vendor.
4. When vendor faxes completed form, SDA checks form for completeness and follows up with vendor contact if necessary.
5. SDA accesses Maintain Vendors screen on Peachtree (Exhibit 3.1.1c) and enters required data from email and New Vendor Form.
6. SDA sight checks the screen to verify that information has been entered accurately and completely.
7. SDA completes any necessary changes and releases the update in Peachtree.
8. SDA sets up a file for the new vendor and files paperwork in folder including:
   - Email from Corporate Sourcing
   - Completed fax form
9. File new vendor folder in Vendor File.

Link(s):
Vendor Tax Reporting Policy – www.ABCcorp.com/Policies/vendortaxpolicy.htm

Screenshots

Screenshots can be incorporated into the manual in a variety of ways. The optimal approach depends on the readers' needs. For compliance related manuals, treating the screenshot as an exhibit is sufficient. For training and operational manuals, the screenshot should be incorporated into the procedure. If the procedure details steps related to a screenshot, we will incorporate callout boxes numbered to match the steps of the procedure. Examples of different ways to integrate screenshots into a procedure are provided in Appendix 5: Sample Procedures with Screenshots.

After you have identified, collected and organized all the exhibits and appendices, you are ready to publish the manual!

Recap:

Thoughtful organization of the manual to promote ease of use and updates will enhance the value of the manual as a resource to your organization.

Utilizing a hub-and-spoke structure facilitates access and maintenance of the manual. The introductory sections and Procedures section are the hub of the manual. The various exhibits and appendices are treated as spokes linked into the hub.

Publishing a Manual

Although organizations are adopting technologies for publishing manuals electronically, we find people even in the most technologically sophisticated organizations who prefer hard copies of manuals. We try to discourage printing manuals, as the information in most manuals can become stale fairly quickly. We highly recommend keeping track of all hard copies which are distributed so that they can be easily recalled when needed.

The presentation of a manual influences its value as an asset to the organization. A well-presented manual is easy on the eye and easy to use. Typos and inconsistencies in the manual may be overlooked by some readers but may lead others to question the accuracy of the content.

This chapter covers publication using the various publishing media. Before publication in any medium, you need to do a final review, or scrub, of the manual.

Final Scrub

The purpose of the final scrub is to trap and correct any typos, grammatical errors, inconsistencies and formatting issues in the manual. Since the manual may be fairly long, as well as heavily structured and formatted, chances are that you will find more than a few errors.

Editing

The document should be put through a rigorous editing process. The editing process should uncover:

- Typos

- Grammatical errors

- Unclear descriptions

- Run-on sentences

- Violations of the rules for writing effective procedures (input→ process→ output)

- Trash (e.g., notes you placed in the text as reminders for yourself which need to be removed)

Since you have been living with the manual for at least several weeks, it may be beneficial, if possible, to assign the edit process to another staff member. Another set of eyes will sometimes catch issues that the writer misses.

There are many fine books available on the subject of editing, so we will not be covering this subject in depth. If writing is not your strong suit, we recommend obtaining a book devoted to the subject.

Formatting

Whether you used your organization's standard formatting templates or our suggested templates, your manual is probably highly formatted. Review the hub of the manual (the narrative introductory sections and the Procedures section) for any formatting inconsistencies including:

- Spacing inconsistencies
  - Between sections and paragraphs
  - In sentences
  - In procedures headers and titles
  - In tabs
  - Between a number or bullet point and the text
- Numbering errors
  - Skipped numbers
  - Repeated numbers
  - Errors in exhibit numbers referencing sections or procedures
  - Errors in appendix numbers
  - Errors in table of contents numbers
- Bullet point inconsistencies
  - In size and type of bullet
  - In spacing

See Appendix 4: Formatting and Review Standards for formatting and reviewing issues that we typically encounter.

Consistency

The manual may contain other inconsistencies, which may be minor or major. A few years ago, we packaged up a compliance related manual for one of our clients who trusted us so strongly that he felt comfortable signing off on our manuals without a thorough review. As he flipped through the manual, one appendix caught his eye. He immediately realized that the information in the appendix was incorrect. He got very upset, because he thought he needed to thoroughly review all the past manuals we had developed for him as well as any future manuals. We had made an unfortunate but avoidable mistake in packaging the manual that almost resulted in the loss of a key client. We had included the wrong appendix in the manual.

To ensure consistency, check:

- Names, particularly titles, department names and names of appendices. An appendix should be referenced by the same name consistently throughout the manual.

- Acronyms. Our rule is to first use the full name followed by the acronym in parentheses (e.g., "Internal Revenue Service (IRS)") and use the acronym thereafter. While you may not want to follow this rule, we recommend selecting a convention and applying it consistently.

- Reference numbers on exhibits and appendices.

- The exhibits and appendices themselves to ensure you have the correct exhibit or appendix.

- Section titles and numbers. Make sure that all references to section titles and numbers are accurate throughout the manual, including in the table of contents.

The Final Touches

Now that you have performed your final checks of the files and made all your final corrections (or so you hope!), there are three items that should be the last tasks performed before publishing the manual.

1. Remove "Draft" from all pages of the manual, including the cover page.

2. Change the date on the manual (in the document header) to be static rather than an automatic date function. This way, any printout of the manual (even a manual printed a year after publication) will show the publication date rather than the current date. An incorrect date on the manual would be misleading to the user.

3. Update the table of contents! In making all of your final corrections, there is a good chance that something in the TOC will need to be updated.

You are now ready to assemble the manual.

Hard Copy Publication

Now that you have scrubbed your final documents, it's time to put them together and publish a hard copy of the manual. We recommend an appropriate-sized three-ring binder. A binder facilitates making changes later on, as it is easy to add and remove pages from a binder. We also recommend using tabs to separate the various sections of the manual to make it easy for users to find the material they are looking for.

The Hub (Main Body)

The first step in publishing a final hard copy of the manual is to print the hub, that is, the main body of the document (i.e., Introduction, Roles and Responsibilities, Procedures). Once you've printed the document, review the document again, as there are certain issues that are easier to identify on a printed copy than on an electronic file. For example:

- Misplaced page breaks
- Inconsistencies in font size or type
- Highlighting that was meant to be removed
- Page numbering mistakes

If necessary, make any changes to the final electronic files, rerun the table of contents and reprint. Once you are satisfied with the printed copy, hole punch and put it in the binder, placing each section's pages behind the appropriate tabs.

The Spokes (Reference Material)

It is now time to print out all the exhibits for the manual. If you have any exhibits in hard copy, have a final copy of those ready. At this time, you will also print the table of contents for the Exhibits section. Again, perform a final review of the printed exhibits, as certain issues may be more evident on the printed copy than the electronic copy. For example:

- Clarity, particularly with colored or shaded areas

- Size and placement of the number reference in the upper left corner

- Additional sheets that may or may not be needed

Check that all exhibits are accounted for by comparing the exhibit to the Exhibits section table of contents and to the section of the manual where the exhibit is referenced. Once all exhibits are accounted for and you are satisfied with the printed copies of the exhibits, hole punch them and put them in the binder behind the Exhibits tab, with the Exhibits table of contents as the first page.

Next, print any appendices (such as policies, regulations or other references) necessary for the manual. As stated earlier, we recommend including a link to a website wherever possible for appendices to facilitate maintenance and extend the life of your manual.

If you do have links (typically Web addresses) for all of your appendices, then you can include the link next to the appendix name on the table of contents for the Appendices section. In this case, the Appendices table of contents would be all you would need to print out for the section. It is important that you check all of the links right before publishing the manual to ensure that they are working, because these links may change.

If you must print some or all of the appendices, perform the same review of the printed appendices as mentioned for the exhibits above. If some of the appendices are large, you may want to consider printing them out double sided. If you decide to do this and you are going to have copies made of the manual, you must make sure to tell the copying company/department about the double-sided pages. This is an easy place for an error to occur, and you have worked too hard on the manual for a slipup so close to the final product.

Once you are satisfied with the printed copies of the appendices, hole punch them and incorporate them into the binder behind the Appendices tab, with the Appendices section table of contents as the first page. We also suggest using numbered tabs to separate the appendices, as they are usually several pages in length.

If you have a mix of links and printed documents for your Appendices section, we recommend putting each appendix behind its own numbered tab. For the appendices that are links to websites, simply put the title of the appendix followed by the link on the printed page, and insert the page behind the appropriate numbered tab.

Make sure to reconcile the Appendices section table of contents to each numbered tab to ensure that the correct appendix is behind the appropriate numbered tab.

The Finishing Touches

Now that you have the body of the document and the appendices assembled in your binder, include a professional-looking cover page for the front cover of the binder and spine.

The cover should be printed in color and include the following:

- Organization name and logo, if appropriate
- Title of the manual (i.e., department name)
- Date published (typically, month and year)
- Type of documentation (i.e., user manual, policies and procedures)
- Your company's name and logo if you are an outside consultant
- Other pertinent information if necessary (i.e., region, parent or sub company, version number)

The spine should also be in color and should typically include the following:

- Organization name and logo, if appropriate
- Title of the manual (i.e., department name)

- Type of documentation (i.e., user manual, policies and procedures)

After one final flip through the manual (perhaps just because you are feeling a little neurotic), you are ready to print the manual.

Making Copies

Now that you have a final document, the next step is to make the appropriate number of copies. The sponsor will tell you how many copies they need. We also recommend making one or two copies for yourself, because people will inevitably come back to you asking for additional copies, and it is much easier to get additional copies made if you have a copy at hand.

Once you know how many copies are needed, there are several ways to get the copies made. We will go from least attractive to most attractive:

- Make the copies yourself – This is very time consuming and probably not the best use of your time.

- Printing vendor (e.g., Staples) – This option is better than doing it yourself, but we all know the feeling you get when you hand over your final product to an outside company. If you use this option, we recommend that you make two copies of the final product before giving one to the vendor for duplication. That way, you have one intact copy, just in case.

- Organization's internal copy or print department – This is the best option and will be more cost effective since the department is internal to the organization.

Give the final manual binder to the printing service, and request that identical copies be made, including color and double-sided printing where necessary. Depending on the printing service, you may have to provide some of the materials (e.g., binder, tabs). Discuss this with the printing service beforehand.

When you receive the copies from the printing service, you will need to do what we refer to as a final "flip through" to ensure that the printing service has assembled the copies correctly and re-assembled the original correctly. Here are examples of common issues with manuals received from the printing service:

- Color cover and spine in each binder may be missing

- Pages may be missing (look at page numbers)

- Blank pages may have been added to the binder

- Pages may be out of order

- Exhibits (including the Exhibits table of contents) may be missing or out of order

- Appendices (including the Appendices table of contents) may be missing or out of order

- Appendices may be behind the wrong numbered tabs

- Pages that were to be two sided may not have been copied that way

- Exhibits and appendices may be unclear or illegible

- Tabs may be incorrect or unclear

If any issues are discovered, determine whether it is easier to fix them yourself or to return the copies to the printing service. Once you are satisfied with the final manuals, you are ready to distribute them.

Soft Copy Publication

If the manual is being published in soft copy format only, the publishing process is not as extensive as the hard copy publication process. Once you have completed the final scrub, you need to incorporate the exhibits and appendices into the main document file.

You can incorporate exhibits into the main document file in a number of ways. If there are not a lot of exhibits and the exhibit files are not very large, we recommend attaching the exhibit files as file links on the Exhibits section table of contents page, next to the name of the exhibit. If, however, the exhibit files are very large or there are just too many, it may make sense to package the exhibit files separately in a folder or zip file. Make sure the exhibits are clearly numbered and named so that there is no confusion as to which exhibit applies to a particular reference in the manual.

Sample Exhibit Files:

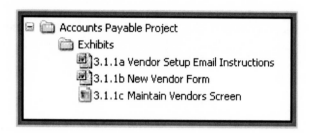

A word of caution when incorporating exhibit files: We mentioned earlier that you must make sure that any sensitive information on an exhibit is redacted. This is easily done for a printed copy, but you must be very careful with electronic exhibit files you attach to your manual. There are many places for sensitive information to be hidden in a file. For example:

- Check document headers and footers.

- Check the file properties.

- For Excel files, check for data on other tabs or hidden cells.

- For PowerPoint files, check the "Notes" view for additional information.

If all the appendices for the manual have links to the appropriate references (usually Web addresses), they will just be included in the Appendices section table of contents. If you have appendix files that need to be included in the manual, attach the appendix files in the same manner as you attached the exhibits above.

Once you have prepared your final document(s), you have to decide how you want to present the final file to the project sponsor. We recommend creating a PDF file, or another type of flat read-only file. However, if the sponsor will be maintaining the document, a read-only file would not be effective. In that case, we recommend providing the sponsor with a password-protected file to limit the number of people that would be able to make changes. The file name for the final file should contain the word "FINAL" and the date.

Publication on a Web-based System

Publishing the manual on a Web-based system may ultimately be the best course of action as far as maintaining the manual (this will be discussed further in Chapter 4 – Change Management). Publishing the manual on a system raises a different set of challenges.

First, you will need to upload your content to the system. Depending on the system, populating the system with the main document content may take some time. The best systems will typically require each section to be uploaded separately in order to keep extensive audit trails. This requirement may lengthen the population process but has advantages in the long run in terms of maintenance and audit history.

Next, you will need to upload the exhibits and appendices, which may be files or links to websites. The best systems allow you to upload the reference material to a central location on the system and then link the references into various sections of the manual. This facilitates maintenance and distribution of the exhibits and appendices.

Once all of your data has been uploaded and linked on the system, you should do one final review to see how the content looks on the system. Then, you are ready to provide users with access to the manual on the system. The best systems allow you to choose different permission levels for different viewers (i.e., read only, full edit access, etc.).

You are now ready to release the final manual on the system. Save the source document you used to populate the system for historical reference purposes.

Recap:

The final scrub during the publishing process is an extremely important step in the creation of a manual. This is the last chance to check for editing, formatting and consistency issues before presenting the final product to the sponsor. A well-presented manual is easy on the eye and easy to use.

The manual will be published as a hard copy, as a soft copy or on a Web-based system. Each way poses certain publishing challenges. Using the hub-and-spoke methodology described in the previous chapter, however, should facilitate the publishing process no matter which medium you decide to use.

Make sure to clearly name/label all documents used for the final publishing of the manual.

Distribution

Congratulations! Your manual is packaged up and ready to be released. Now it's time for you to get some recognition for all your hard work.

Publicizing the Manual

We strongly suggest that you plan a "release party" to introduce the manual to its audience.   This should be coupled with broadcast announcements, preferably via email, to interested stakeholders within the larger organization.

Coordinate with the project sponsor to invite key stakeholders to a brief meeting. If possible, arrange to have refreshments available. The tone of the meeting should be upbeat and celebratory. Regardless of the medium used to publish the manual, the agenda for the meeting should include:

- Purpose and scope of the manual

- How the manual will help the stakeholders (the WIIFM)

- Organization of contents (i.e., how to use the manual)

- How to access the manual

- How the manual will be updated (see Chapter 4 – Change Management)

Show the manual to the meeting participants by providing hard copies or by walking them through a presentation of the soft copy or Web-based system. Invite them to provide feedback on the manual.

Hard Copy Distribution

Managing the distribution of hard copies of a manual requires planning. Ideally, whenever the manual is updated, any hard copies that have been distributed should be retrieved and replaced with the update. Maintaining a history of stakeholders who receive copies of the manual facilitates the retrieval process up to a point. We find that stakeholders move to other positions and that hard copies frequently get lost.

To minimize the risk of a "lost" outdated copy of the manual being used by a stakeholder who assumes the information is reliable, be sure you have included the date on the cover and every page of a hard copy manual. It's also helpful to include an instruction for obtaining updated copies, both on the cover and within the manual. If it's possible to maintain a centralized copy of the manual electronically on a shared drive, the address should be included in the instruction.

These issues all speak to the weaknesses of hard copy manuals. They are inherently difficult to control and often end up outside the organization. A few years ago, we were working with a client to develop several manuals, including a sales manual. The manager of the sales group insisted that she had a manual. When we pressed her to show us the manual, she showed us a sales manual from her previous employer.

There is a strong case to be made for electronic solutions for distributing manuals and managing updates. We will cover various solutions in Chapter 4 – Change Management.

Soft Copy Distribution

Soft copy distribution solves some of the problems attributed to hard copy manuals, depending on where the soft copy is published. Options include:

- On a shared drive

- On an intranet

- On a document management system (e.g., SharePoint)

Wherever the soft copy resides, stakeholders will need to know how to access the manual. In addition to the introductory meeting and announcements regarding the manual, consider introductions to new stakeholders.

For soft copies housed on shared drives, access to the shared drive may be a problem for some stakeholders. If it's not possible to provide access to the shared drive for some stakeholders, consider publishing the manual on additional shared drives.

We also recommend that the cover and every page of the soft copy manual be dated. The soft copy should also indicate the name/department of the owner/contact for the manual.

Distribution via a Web-Based System

In addition to reducing packaging costs associated with producing hard copy manuals, Web-based systems can eliminate the problems inherent with maintaining hard copies of manuals. Depending on the system, access to manuals can be more flexibly controlled. The best systems facilitate updates and their communication to stakeholders.

Web-based systems will be covered in more depth in Chapter 4 – Change Management.

Recap:

A release party is the best way to introduce the manual to its audience. The agenda for this meeting would include:

- Purpose and scope of the manual

- How the manual will help the stakeholders (the WIIFM)

- Organization of contents (i.e., how to use the manual)

- How to access the manual

- How the manual will be updated

Distribution of the manual to its intended audience is then accomplished by giving out hard copies of the manual; posting the soft copy of the manual on a shared drive, intranet or document management system; or uploading the manual to a Web-based policies and procedures system.

If you distribute hard copies of a manual, it is important for change management purposes to track who has received the copies.

Project Closure

Now that you have successfully completed your policies and procedures manual, make sure you have tied up all the loose ends. This is a good time to ensure that you have updated all of your project tools and retained them in an accessible place for reference purposes.

Acknowledgements

At the end of a project, it is a good idea to call or email the sponsor and any other people who were particularly helpful during the course of the project. This may include SMEs, administrative assistants, IT resources or even the printing service. This acknowledgement lets people know that you understand how busy they are and that you appreciate their time and help during the project. This leaves them with a good feeling, and they may be more inclined to help you with any follow-ups that are needed in the future. Now is also a good time to ask for any feedback on the project and solicit references. Alternatively, you can acknowledge people in a project closure or hand-off meeting with the project sponsor and select stakeholders.

If you worked with a team of your own to develop the manual, be sure to acknowledge all of their hard work that contributed to the successful completion of the project. You can do this in a number of ways, such as:

- Lunch or dinner
- Email recognition
- Rewards

It is important to recognize a job well done!

Project Workbook

Now that you have completed the project, it is time to clean up. You probably have many folders with notes, emails, and documents lying around on your desk. This is the time to review all this material and decide what can be thrown out and what needs to be saved.

A good rule of thumb as to what should be saved and incorporated into the Project Workbook is:

- Anything with handwritten notes on it

- Anything that contains a sign-off or verification

- Any documents for which you do not have electronic copies

Ensure that all sign-offs and verifications are maintained in the Project Workbook for future reference. This may entail printing out email sign-offs.

You should check the Document Tracker and return any documents that need to be returned. Also, print the final Document Tracker and Meetings Tracker, and incorporate these into the workbook for reference purposes.

Electronic Files

It is a good idea to review and organize the electronic files and folders where you have saved the working and final documents. At this time, you can determine if any files can be deleted. Be sure file names are clear, so that files are easy to find and you can easily tell which documents are the final documents versus earlier drafts. Emails that need to be saved should be organized and saved to a particular email folder as well.

Sample File Folder Structure and Files for Accounts Payable Project:

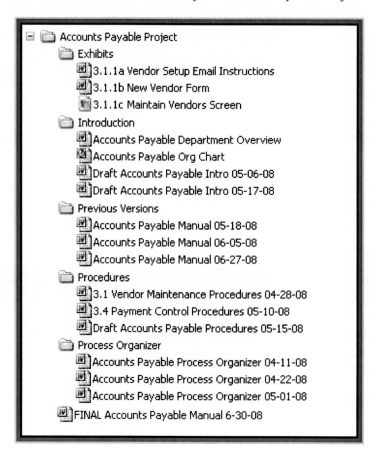

Recap:

Update and finalize all of your project management tools, including tracking sheets and the Project Workbook, which should include:

- Anything with handwritten notes on it
- Anything that contains a sign-off or verification
- Any documents for which you do not have electronic copies

Organize electronic files and folders, and label documents in a clear and concise way. Get rid of any unnecessary files or papers.

Thank people for their help during the project and acknowledge team members (if you were working with a team) for a job well done.

Chapter 4
Change Management

Challenges in Manual Maintenance

Before you embark on developing a manual (assuming that you have read this before you've developed the manual!), it's wise to consider change management issues. Depending on your industry and the subject matter of your manual, the manual could be stale shortly after it is published. As with any big-ticket item you purchase, ease of maintenance is an important consideration. Keeping manuals up to date is sometimes viewed as punishing and unrewarding. The task is particularly burdensome if the manuals are maintained in hard copy format and somewhat less burdensome for soft copies.

Manual maintenance presents several challenges. The first, but not the least, of the challenges is collecting the information needed to keep the manual current. Ideally, the information should automatically route to the owner of the manual.

This leads us to the second challenge: identifying an owner for the manual. Depending on your role, you may not want to be the owner. If there is one key SME, that individual may be the logical candidate, given that they will probably be aware of most of the necessary changes. No matter what the medium, effective maintenance requires clear assignment of ownership responsibility for the manual and management oversight. Lacking management commitment and oversight, the manual will quickly lose its value as an asset to the organization.

Updating the manual itself can be messy, depending on how the manual is organized. If you follow our recommendations on manual design and organization, updates should be less of a challenge.

If a manual is published in hard copy, all the issued manuals should be rounded up and re-issued when there are updates. This can be time consuming, and some manuals may escape the round-up process. It's generally easier to handle updates if the manual is exclusively in soft copy on one or more shared drives.

Whether the manual has been published in hard or soft copy, all stakeholders may need to be notified of changes, depending on the impact of the changes. You can use email communications to do this, but in most organizations it's sometimes unclear whether an email communication has been received and read.

In this chapter, we outline strategies for facilitating the change management process for each of the publishing options:

- Hard copies
- Soft copies
- Web-based systems

In general, none of our suggested strategies will be effective if your organization does not value knowledge management and/or staff compliance with policies and procedures. Why is this? Each of the strategies requires an investment in resources. Since the payback on an investment in knowledge management and/or staff compliance tends to be difficult to quantify in hard currency, many organizations fail to make the investment.

Unless you are part of a central group responsible for managing the organization's procedural knowledge, the change management requirement should be discussed with the project sponsor before the manual is developed. If the manual needs to be written to meet a requirement and there is no plan for maintaining the manual, consider scaling the project to minimally meet the requirement.

Hard Copy Manuals

By now, you have probably concluded that hard copy manuals present the greatest change management challenges. While you may expect that the hard copy medium is the most economical, in the long term it is both labor intensive and skill intensive.

In our discussion of distribution, we indicated that a distribution list should be maintained for hard copies. This list should include the name and department of everyone who receives a copy of the manual, along with the date they received it. Ideally, as stakeholders change their roles and departments reorganize, the owner of the manual will update the list. Ongoing maintenance of the list is one reason it's beneficial to keep the distribution list short.

Since hard copy manuals will need to be recalled for updates, it makes sense to establish a schedule of updates. The schedule should be aligned with the organization's environment and needs. We recommend at least an annual update and interim updates as needed. This way, if major changes have occurred, the manual can be updated fairly quickly. A calendar of updates, including when the update was made and by whom, should be maintained.

Updates to hard copy manuals can be made as addendums, or the manual content can actually be modified. Addendums may reference the section being updated and indicate the change, or they may provide an updated replacement page. The use of addendums is less labor intensive and provides the reader with the benefit of being able to access the original content. If, however, the addendum is lost or overlooked by the reader, the content they are reading will be unreliable.

Actually recalling issued manuals and completing the update process centrally is more time consuming but provides greater reliability. The manual owner can review the condition of the manual and replace worn and torn pages. Also, this process allows the owner to speak with users about the manual and get feedback about how frequently they consult the manual, what's helpful and how the manual might be enhanced. The date of the update should be incorporated into the manual, along with the name of a contact person.   After the manual is updated, the manual owner should update the central history record accordingly.

Finally, a process for collecting updated data will need to be established. Depending on the nature of the manual, data may need to be collected from several sources:

- The SMEs
- General announcements of organizational changes
- Interface departments
- Policy setting groups
- News media

A process will need to be designed and implemented for receiving updates from each of these sources.   If a regular update schedule has been established, much of this information should be collected during the update cycle.   For interim major changes, you'll need to set up a process that ensures you are advised timely.

Soft Copy Manuals

Soft copies of manuals are much less resource intensive to update than hard copies, because the manual is stored in one place (or a handful of places if on several shared drives). As with hard copy manuals, a history of changes should be incorporated into the soft copy manual. This can be a page preceding the table of contents. The name of the individual responsible for the update should be included on the page.

Actually making changes is simplified for a soft copy manual, but, depending on the materiality, many changes will still need to be communicated to stakeholders. In most cases, email is the preferred medium for this communication. If possible, track receipt of the email by requesting a read receipt. If a change to a manual is material, we recommend printing out the receipts as an audit trail. This may seem like "overkill," but in many organizations we hear of breakdowns resulting from incomplete communications. If your organization is small, a phone call may be preferable.

As with hard copy manuals, an update schedule and process should be established for soft copy manuals. A process should also be set up to advise the manual owner of significant changes that occur between scheduled updates.

Web-based Systems

Web-based systems for managing policies and procedures address the challenges inherent in distributing and maintaining policies and procedures. Requests from our consulting clients for a "living manual" led us to develop a system, FirmCover®, several years ago. These systems should not be confused with document management systems. Policies and procedures systems are designed primarily for communicating policies, procedures and other requirements and for facilitating updates.

Most policies and procedures systems on the market today offer similar functionality. Some are more user-friendly and flexible than others, and some incorporate specific features which may be attractive based on your organization's needs. Basic features offered by most systems include:

- A central repository for housing policies and procedures

- Controlled access

- A workflow approval process for authoring and/or managing updates

- Communication of changes to stakeholders

- Audit trails of changes and/or versioning

Before recommending a policies and procedures system to your organization's management, consider the environment and culture. The companies we find most open to considering policies and procedures systems tend to like technology solutions and/or incur risks if policies and procedures are not communicated timely to staff. Organizations needing a risk management solution tend to be in highly regulated, complex and/or dynamic industries.

Since the firm will incur hard dollar costs for developing or purchasing a system, you'll probably need to present a cost-benefit analysis. The costs will include soft dollar costs for implementing and managing the system. Many of the savings for implementing a policies and procedures system may not be obvious or easily quantifiable, so it may be tricky to get your arms around total saves.

Even with a policies and procedures system, manuals and other content will still require updates. Most systems also require an administrator to manage user permissions, training and archiving. Some of our clients opt to have us handle the administration and management of the system.

Congratulations! We hope that we have provided you with "food for thought"! Before you begin developing your manual, consider the change management aspects we have outlined.

Recap:

Discuss change management of the manual with the project sponsor before you begin the manual writing process, as this consideration may influence how you choose to distribute and maintain the manual. No matter which medium you choose, effective maintenance requires clear assignment of ownership responsibility for the manual and management oversight.

Also, regardless of the medium, a schedule should be set for conducting regular updates. A process will need to be developed for collecting, incorporating and distributing the updated content. A process for notifying all stakeholders of changes will also need to be put in place.

Web-based systems are typically the best choice from a change management and ease of maintenance perspective.

Chapter 5
Policies

Overview

In the Introduction, we outlined some of the differences between policies and procedures, along with documentation challenges. In this chapter, we would like to share some strategies for facilitating the processes of developing and updating policies.

Most organizations house the responsibility for developing policies with internal policy setting groups and/or subject matter experts, such as Safety and Security for security related policies. Policies generally require sign-off by multiple stakeholders. The requirement for multiple sign-offs on the entire policy generally slows down the development process. There tends to be a direct correlation between the amount of organizational change required by a policy and the time it takes to get the policy approved. It's best to make it as easy as possible for stakeholders to say "yes."

In general, the same rules that apply to the rapid development of manuals apply to the rapid development of policies. Let's take a look at how the Four Golden Rules apply to developing policies.

1. Never, never start from scratch.
Since policies require working with a team or committee or coordinating with stakeholders, it is critical to use what we refer to as a Strawman to get the process started. For policies, it's easy to find precedents to use as starting points. These could be standard templates the organization already uses to

document policies, standard policies on the topic available on the Internet, or existing policies in your organization that may be similar to the new policy. If the organization is global, there may be a global policy in place on the subject that can be used as the starting point for localization.

Finding and using precedents (conventions or practices already vetted) is a powerful technique for jumpstarting the policy development process. People generally find it harder to say "no" to precedents.

If you are charged with updating a policy, we recommend first reviewing the policy, even though the policy is already in place. Try to identify aspects of the policy which may warrant updating based on changes in regulations, industry guidelines or other environmental factors before you meet with the team or individual stakeholders.

2.   Always, always work from the top down.

If policies are to be developed rapidly, it's essential that the committee or stakeholders first agree on the purpose and scope of the policy. Details on how the policy will be implemented, who will be responsible, etc. must be viewed as secondary. Focusing on details before the purpose and scope are nailed down may lead to disagreements, delays and a loss of productivity.

3.   Organizers rule!

While policies tend to be shorter than a procedures manual, an effective organizer will facilitate management of the project as well as readability and maintenance of the policy. Your organization may already have a standard format for policies, but you will have some flexibility in how you modularize the project to facilitate completion.

4.   Do it once!

Depending on the policy, re-work can result from disagreement among the committee members and/or stakeholders and a spiral of modifications. Modifications to the policies generally need to be vetted with all the stakeholders. This can lead to more modifications, re-vetting and so on. To avoid re-work, the policy development process needs to be staged carefully.

Designing Policy Organizers

Unless your organization has a standard template for policies, we recommend that your policy contain at least four to five main sections or components:

1. Purpose or Goal of the Policy

2. Scope of the Policy

3. Requirements (e.g., rules)

4. Roles and Responsibilities

5. Related Procedures (will depend on the policy)

This organizer will facilitate overall maintenance of the policy. Generally, the Purpose and Scope section of the policy should not be subject to frequent changes.   The supporting Requirements, Roles and Responsibilities and Related Procedures may need periodic modification; as a result, it works best to house them in separate sections. It may also be beneficial to provide an overview or summary of the policy, depending on the importance and/or length of the policy.

If your organization does not use a standard organizer for policies, the project sponsor of the policy and the team or individual stakeholders should sign off on the organizer you draft. If you obtain verbal sign-offs, follow up with an email confirming the agreed-upon organizer.

Development of Policies

Since the sections or components of a policy are interdependent, we recommend obtaining interim sign-offs on each of the components to accelerate development.   Interim sign-offs help to avoid a spiral of modifications to the policy. For example, if all parties with approval rights over the policy have signed off on the Purpose and Scope of the policy, it will be easier to get their sign-off on the Requirements, Roles and Responsibilities and Related Procedures. Later changes to the Purpose and Scope of the policy to align a policy with a Requirement or Role and Responsibility favored by a given committee/team member or individual stakeholder may open up a "Pandora's box" and delay the development process.

Depending on the organizer for the policy, we recommend structuring the project into at least three sequential stages:

1. Finalization of the Purpose and Scope

2. Development of the Requirements

3. Development of Roles and Responsibilities and Related Procedures

The Purpose and Scope essentially govern the other aspects of the policy. As indicated above, it's critical that the Purpose and Scope are finalized before developing the Requirements, or rules. The Requirements, in turn, govern the Roles and Responsibilities and Related Procedures.   The relationship is analogous to a series of waterfalls.

Waterfall Approach

Purpose

    Scope

        Requirements

            Roles and Responsibilities
and Related Procedures

The same 6 basic Rapid Documentation Steps used for procedures manuals can be utilized for each of the policy development stages with one key modification to step 6.

1. Build a Strawman

2. Collect Information

3. Draft Content

4. Verify Content

5. Modify Content

6. Obtain Sign-off on Content

For policies, two sign-offs are needed:

- The first sign-off is on the key elements to be included in each section.

- The second sign-off is on the actual narrative of the section.

Before you invest time in drafting the narrative of the section, it's essential that all review group members (the team/committee or individual stakeholders) have agreed to the basic elements of the section. Once this agreement has been reached, you can draft the narrative of the section for approval.

Let's run through an example of this approach, focusing on the Purpose section of the policy.

The Purpose, or goal, of the policy is essentially the reason the policy is required. High-level reasons for establishing a policy include:

- A regulatory or industry requirement

- A need to control or reduce risk

- Standardization of practices across the organization to achieve organizational goals

The Purpose should address the macro as well as the specific reasons for the establishment of the policy.

The Scope of the policy specifies what the policy covers (and, in some cases, does not cover) and which groups within the organization the policy governs. The Scope may also include whether the policy supersedes other policies.

The Purpose and Scope can be handled separately (as its own waterfall) or concurrently (a combined waterfall), depending on the policy and its impact on the organization. If the impact of the policy will be significant in terms of expanding roles and responsibilities and creating additional procedures, we recommend aligning the team/committee or individual stakeholders around the Purpose of the policy first and then tackling the Scope.

If you are the SME in a policy setting group, chances are that you have most of the information needed to build a Strawman for the Purpose and Scope of the policy (step 1 of the Rapid Documentation Steps). If you are not the SME, you will need to do some research.

Let's assume that your assignment is to develop a Vendor Management Policy. Your research should include:

- Identifying similar policies within your organization. These may be:

  - Global policies

  - Policies used by other regions

  - Policies used by other groups/divisions within the organization

  - Policies that the new policy may be replacing

- Internet research. Sample policies can frequently be found on the Internet. These can be excellent starting points and can in some cases be used to establish precedents. Universities, government agencies and members of industry groups often share policies online. For example, entering the search term "Vendor Management Policy" in a search engine will bring up sample vendor management policies.

Based on your research, draft a list of bullet points which address the reason for the policy. If there is a regulatory or industry guideline, include it at the top of your list. For example, draft bullet points for the Vendor Management Policy may include:

- Comply with FACT Act of 2003 (if your organization is a bank)
- Standardize requirements for oversight of vendors
- Protect the organization's confidential information

If the policy addresses a regulatory requirement, obtain the requirement and bullet out the key details of the requirement. This summary of the regulatory requirement should be sent to all team/committee members or individual stakeholders as part of the invitation to attend the first meeting.

Set up a meeting with the team/committee, or set up individual meetings with the stakeholders to collect information (step 2). Review the summary of the regulatory requirement, along with any other potential purposes for the policy you have drafted. Solicit additional potential purposes from the group. If you are meeting with a group rather than conducting individual interviews with stakeholders, we recommend capturing the potential purposes for the policy on an easel chart. Upon completion of the "brainstorming" part of the meeting, review the potential purposes and combine similar purposes. Get agreement from the group on the purposes they view as critical.

Draft a summary of the purpose(s) (step 3), and review the draft with the project sponsor (or your manager) (step 4) before circulating the draft to the team/committee or stakeholders for sign-off. The summary should list the purpose and provide background information as appropriate, but the summary should still be in an outline format. It's best not to invest time in drafting the final version until everyone has signed off on the key purpose(s).

Modify the purpose as necessary based on feedback from the members of the review group (step 5).

When everyone has agreed on the purpose(s) (step 6), draft the Purpose section as a narrative. Any changes proposed by members of the review group should be cosmetic. The narrative draft can then be circulated for approval. (Repeat steps 3 through 6 of the Rapid Documentation Steps for the narrative you have drafted.)

Use this approach for each remaining section of the policy.

If at any point you encounter resistance or disagreement, the previously agreed-upon sections should be used as a precedent. Should you encounter stubborn disagreement, the review group should then determine whether they want to open up sections they have previously agreed upon. Unless there was an important oversight (i.e., a good reason for re-visiting the section), most groups will be hesitant to re-open agreed-upon sections.

Recap:

Most policies require sign-off by multiple stakeholders. For policies resulting in a significant impact on the organization, we recommend:

- Adopting the Waterfall Approach to stage the development process.

- Nailing down agreement of key elements of each section (waterfall) prior to drafting the narrative.

A word about additional support for your project...

We have assembled examples of the tools described throughout this guide in the Appendices.

Although this handbook contains much of the information you need to successfully complete your project, please feel free to visit our website at www.btiworld.com for additional support, especially if your situation is complex. We offer training sessions and consultative support.

Appendices

1. Sample Shell Manual
2. Policy/Regulation Matrix Shell
3. Procedure Writing Tips
4. Formatting and Review Standards
5. Sample Procedures with Screenshots

Appendix 1: Sample Shell Manual

ABC Company

Accounts Payable

Policies & Procedures Documentation

Benchmark Technologies International Inc.
www.btiworld.com

November 2008

Table of Contents

Section 1.0 – Introduction

1.1   Why this manual is important

1.2   How to use this manual

1.3   Intended audience

1.4   Department Overview

1.5   Process Overview

1.6   Risk Controls

1.7   Systems

1.8   Regulations and Internal Policies

1.9   Business Continuity

Section 2.0 – Roles and Responsibilities

2.1   Organizational Structure

2.2   Risk Management

2.3   Interfacing Areas

Note: Process Organizer page should be Landscape orientation.

Section 3.0 – Procedures

Accounts Payable Process Organizer

3.1	**Vendor Maintenance**
3.1.1	Set up New Vendor
3.1.2	Modify Vendor Information
3.1.3	Close Vendor Account

3.2	**Invoice Approval**	3.3	**Invoice Payment**	3.4	**Payment Control**
3.2.1	Verify Invoice Approved	3.3.1	Execute Electronic Payment	3.4.1	Reconcile Payables Account
3.2.2	Resolve Unapproved Invoices	3.3.2	Execute Check Payment	3.4.2	Investigate Discrepancies
3.2.3	Resolve Inquiries			3.4.3	Correct Errors

3.5	**Employee Expense Payment**	3.6	**Department Management**
3.5.1	Ensure Expenses Valid	3.6.1	Maintain Records
3.5.2	Resolve Inquiries	3.6.2	Generate Management Reports
3.5.3	Execute Payment		

3.1 Vendor Maintenance

3.1.1 Set up New Vendor

Responsibility:
Involved Parties:
System(s):
Procedures:

Link(s):

3.1   Vendor Maintenance

3.1.2   Modify Vendor Information

Responsibility:
Involved Parties:
System(s):
Procedures:

Link(s):

3.1   Vendor Maintenance

3.1.3   Close Vendor Account

Responsibility:
Involved Parties:
System(s):
Procedures:

Link(s):

Additional procedure pages would follow the same format.

Section 4.0 – Exhibits

List Exhibits in this area.

Section 5.0 – Appendices

List Appendices in this area.

Sample manual header:

Draft Accounts Payable Policies and Procedures Manual	11/21/08

Sample manual footer:

1

Appendix 2: Policy/Regulation Matrix Shell

Summary of Applicable Policies and Regulations Template		
Global / Regional	Regulation / Policy	Reference / Notes
Function Related		
Staff Related		
Operationally Related		

Summary of Applicable Policies Template		
Regulation / Policy	Reference / Notes	Global / Regional
Accounting / Controlling		
Communication / Marketing		
Logistics / Operations		
Human Resources		
IT		
Legal / Compliance / Ethics		
Risk		
Safety and Security		

Appendix 3: Procedure Writing Tips

I. Headings

1. At the top of each page indicate the high level function (2 digit title) and the individual process (3 digit title). If the procedure steps go onto additional pages, repeat this heading structure with "(Continued)" after the Process (3 digit) Title.

2. Complete the following Header Fields after each Process (3 digit or 4 digit) Title as necessary:

   - Primary Owner – Person(s) responsible for completing the process or ensuring the process is performed.

   - Involved Parties – Other person(s) involved in some way in the procedure.

   - Timing – For example, Daily, monthly, etc.; Time of day; Must be done prior to… or after… ; etc.

   - System(s) – List any systems used in performing the process.

3. If necessary, the process may be separated into sub-processes using another title (4 digit) to make the document more manageable. In these cases the Header Fields may be used once prior to the 4 digit titles or after each of the 4 digit titles if the Headers are specific to each.

4. Reasons for separating a process into sub-processes (4 digit titles) include:

   - Different systems are used to perform a process

   - A process is performed differently for different products

   - There are two distinct activities performed for a process

   - A process is performed differently based on timing (i.e., daily vs. monthly)

   - Length of the process

Example:

3.6	**Function Management**
3.6.3	**Manage Records**

Responsibility: Administrative Assistant
System(s): ABC System
Procedures:

3.6.3.1 Manage Records – On Site Filing

    1. Sample step one.
    2. Sample step two.

3.6.3.2 Manage Records – Off Site Archiving

    1. Sample step one.
    2. Sample step two.

II. Procedure Formatting Convention

1. If necessary, an introductory sentence(s) may be added before the numbered procedure steps to provide context or additional information relevant to the process. Introductory text should be formatted in an *italicized font*.

2. Draft procedures use the following numerical structure (sub procedure steps and bulleted lists are used on an as needed basis):
   1. Procedure Step (action taken)
      1. Sub Procedure Step
         - Lists

3. If necessary, sub procedure steps are used to explain actions taken in direct relation to the preceding procedure step or actions taken to complete the preceding procedure step. Additional sub procedure step levels may be added as necessary.

4. Bulleted lists are used when there is a list of items relating to the preceding procedure step (i.e., list of reports, list of fields, list of people, etc.).

5. Restart numbering for each new title (3 digit, 4 digit, etc.).

Example:

3.1   Vendor Maintenance

3.1.1   Set up New Vendor

Responsibility: Static Data Associate (SDA)
Involved Parties: Corporate Sourcing
System(s):   Peachtree
Procedures:

Corporate Sourcing is responsible for approving new vendors. After a new vendor is approved, they advise Accounts Payable of approval and payment terms. Accounts Payable is required to obtain a Tax Identification Number from all vendors.

1. Static Data Associate receives an email instruction (Exhibit 3.1.1a) from Corporate Sourcing to set up a new vendor and reviews email for completeness following up with Corporate Sourcing if necessary.
2. Call vendor contact for additional information and indicate information provided on email from Corporate Sourcing including:
    - Tax identification number (per Vendor Tax Reporting Policy)
    - Payment instructions
    - Ability to send invoice via PDF
    - Fax number
3. Complete fax cover sheet and form (Exhibit 3.1.1b) and fax to new vendor.
4. When vendor faxes completed form, SDA checks form for completeness and follows up with vendor contact if necessary.
5. SDA accesses Maintain Vendors screen on Peachtree (Exhibit 3.1.1c) and enters required data from email and New Vendor Form.
6. SDA sight checks the screen to verify that information has been entered accurately and completely.
7. SDA completes any necessary changes and releases the update in Peachtree.
8. SDA sets up a file for the new vendor and files paperwork in folder including:
    - Email from Corporate Sourcing
    - Completed fax form
9. File new vendor folder in Vendor File.

III. Procedure Writing Convention

1. Each procedure step should be written in a **crisp, clear, concise** style.

2. The following are general rules to be followed in drafting the procedures:

   - Each process should indicate inputs and where the input is received from (the customer, a report, another department)

   - Each process should indicate outputs and to whom or where the output is sent

   - Generally, each process should contain at least one control point

   - Each procedure step should describe one task/activity

   - The job position (e.g. Manager) responsible for performing the activity should be indicated for each procedure step unless only one position is responsible for the entire process

   - Procedure steps should be written with an active voice (not passive)

3. There are often parts of a process that do not require an action by the person performing the procedure, but are necessary to include in the procedure. This information should not be included as a procedure step. The following examples show how this information can be included in a procedure:

   - Include in parentheses within a procedure step.

   Example:

1. Payroll Specialist reviews shift differential documentation <u>(indicating the number of days for which a shift differential should be applied and the appropriate percentage, 10% or 15%)</u> received from the department managers via email.

- Include as a bulleted note after the procedure step.

Example:

---

1. Upon terminating a trade, the Trader enters the termination fee in ABC system.
   - The termination fee amount is automatically fed from ABC System to XYZ System for processing.

- Include in the italics background prior to the procedure steps.

Example:

An active investor with web access to ABC system is able to update their contact details themselves. Alternatively, the investor may contact Operations to update their details.

1. Operations updates the investor's contact details in ABC system when notified of a change by the investor.

---

4. Review the draft procedures for completeness, accuracy, and logical flow.

5. Revise the draft procedures as needed.

Appendix 4: Formatting and Review Standards

Final Review for All Procedural Benchmarking Manuals
When creating a new manual, a previously completed manual should be used, if possible, to create a shell document for the new manual so that it will already contain all of the formatting mentioned in this document. When adding additional titles or sections to a manual, copying and pasting similar titles and sections is preferred. This will significantly reduce the chance of inconsistency in manuals.

Pre Duplication Review
Paragraph markings should be enabled during all reviews.

1. Overall Manual Review
    1. Grammatical check (use Microsoft grammar checker)
    2. Spelling check (use Microsoft spelling checker)
    3. Check for people's names throughout the document
    4. Punctuation
        - Period at the end of every procedure
        - Parentheses and quotation marks have an open: (" and close:) "
    5. Always update Table of Contents before final print
        - Always choose "Update Entire Table"
    6. Ensure tab labels are in correct order (if hard copy)

2. Headers/Footers
    1. Header
        - Title of document 16 pt at Left throughout the document
        - Date 10 pt at Right
    2. Footer
        - Page numbers continuous throughout the document
        - 10 pt in center of page

3. Introduction/Roles and Responsibilities (R&R)
    1. Spacing
        - Look for extra spaces between words

- 1 space (return) between Section Heading and 2 digit heading
- 2 spaces (returns) between 2 digit title sections
  - 1 space (return) after 2 digit title before text
- 1 space (return) between 3 digit title sections
  - No space (return) after 3 digit title before text
- Tab to 0.5 between number and name of 2 digit and 3 digit headings

2. Fonts
   - Entire document in Arial
   - We suggest creating the following font styles in Word:
     - *Style Heading 1*: Section Heading – 16 pt
     - *Style Heading 1a:* 2 Digit Heading – 12 pt, Bold
     - *Style Heading 1b:* 3 Digit Heading – 10 pt, Bold
     - Same for any subsequent headings except don't use style
   - Text – 10 pt

3. Bullets (Introduction/Roles and Responsibilities only)
   - Round, 8 pt
   - Bullets at 0.5 indent, text at 0.75
     - Same indents for numbering

Section 1.0 – Introduction

1.1   Why this manual is important

Payroll Processing is responsible for all aspects of operational and financial control relating to payroll generation, benefit payments and associated accounting activities. Payroll Processing is part of the Human Resources Group. The Group is based in New York, NY. For more detail relating to the Group's activities, see Overview of Activities.

1.2   How to use this manual

The information in this text is meant to provide the user with a reference to the procedures followed by Payroll Processing. This manual is divided into three main sections. Sections 1.0 and 2.0 provide the reader with overviews of the Business and its organization. Procedures, as well as references to exhibits, critical regulations and policies are included in Section 3.0. Section 4.0 contains flowcharts. Exhibits can be found in Section 5.0.

1.3   Intended Audience

This manual is intended for the use of all employees of Payroll Processing and related areas and for distribution and use by any internal auditors and external regulatory authorities.

1.4   Overview of Payroll Processing Activities

1.4.1   Overview of Activities

Payroll Processing ensures that quality control is provided over the payroll process and associated payment, reporting and accounting processes for the firm. The unit handles various types of special payments including bonuses, tuition reimbursements, severance, employee referrals and club reimbursements. Payroll Processing also ensures that the firm complies with payroll related legal, regulatory and tax reporting requirements.

In order to manage the payroll function cost-effectively, many of the payroll processing activities have been outsourced to ADP, a large established U.S.-based provider of payroll services.

4. Process Organizer
    1. Page Landscaped facing out
    2. Ensure Section Heading – 16 pt (*Style: Heading 1*) – is on this page
    3. Ensure Title is Bold, 14 pt, Centered
    4. Ensure that 2 digit numbers and titles are Bold, 10 pt
    5. Ensure that 3 digit numbers and titles are Normal, 10 pt
    6. Check sequence of numbers
    7. Ensure components of organizer correspond to actual procedures
    8. Process Organizer only goes to 3 digit level
    9. The core procedures for the group should be one connected gray box
    10. Other boxes should be separated, not colored

Section 3.0 – Procedures

Accounts Payable Process Organizer

3.1	Vendor Maintenance
3.1.1	Set up New Vendor
3.1.2	Modify Vendor Information
3.1.3	Close Vendor Account

3.2	Invoice Approval	3.3	Invoice Payment	3.4	Payment Control
3.2.1	Verify Invoice Approved	3.3.1	Execute Electronic Payment	3.4.1	Reconcile Payables Account
3.2.2	Resolve Unapproved Invoices	3.3.2	Execute Check Payment	3.4.2	Investigate Discrepancies
3.2.3	Resolve Inquiries			3.4.3	Correct Errors

3.5	Employee Expense Payment	3.6	Department Management
3.5.1	Ensure Expenses Valid	3.6.1	Maintain Records
3.5.2	Resolve Inquiries	3.6.2	Generate Management Reports
3.5.3	Execute Payment		

5. Procedures
    1. Spacing/Fonts
        - Look for extra spaces between words
        - We suggest creating the following styles in Word for the titles:
            - *Style Procedure 1a:* 2 digit title – 14 pt, tab to 1.0 between number and name of title
            - *Style Procedure 1b*: 3 digit title – 14 pt, tab to 1.0 between number and name of title
            - *Style Procedure Phony*: 14 pt, tab to 1.0 between number and name of title
        - Each Procedure page should be set up as follows:
            - 10 pt space (return)
            - 2 digit title – 14 pt, tab to 1.0 between number and name of title (*Style: Procedure 1a*)
            - 10 pt space (return)
            - Line
            - 10 pt space (return)
            - 3 digit title – 14 pt, tab to 1.0 between number and name of title (*Style: Procedure 1b*)
            - 10 pt space (return)
            - Line
            - 10 pt space (return)
            - Responsibility, System(s), Procedures – Bold, 10 pt, tab to 1.0 for text
            - 10 pt space (return)
            - Italics – full justification
            - 10 pt space (return)
            - Procedures
            - 3 10 pt spaces (returns)
            - Link Box – full justification (ensure that box is full width of page)
    2. Numbering
        - Check sequence of numbers
        - Check for font, bold, italics of numbers
        - First level
            - Numbers (1.) at 0 indent, text at 0.25
        - Second level
            - Numbers (1.) at 0.25 indent, text at 0.5

- Third level
  - Bullets at 0.5 indent, text at 0.75
  - Font – Symbol, 8 pt
- Check for additional levels as needed using similar increments.

3. 4 Digit Heading
   - 14 pt, tab to 1.0 between number and name of title (*Style: Procedure Phony*)
   - Repeat 3 digit title with a dash then subtitle
   - May be before or after italics, or Responsibility, System(s), Procedures
   - 10 pt space (return) before and after heading
   - 2 10 pt spaces (returns) between 4 digit procedure sections
   - 3 10 pt spaces (returns) after final 4 digit procedure section before Link Box

4. Link Box
   - Only at 3 digit procedure level (after final 4 digit procedure)
   - No space (return) after Link(s) heading in box
   - Space (return) at end of box
   - Ensure that box is full width of page

5. Procedures Continuing onto Multiple Pages
   - Ensure that every page has the 2 digit and 3 digit titles at the top of the page
   - 3 digit titles that go onto multiple pages should have "(Continued)" added to the title
   - *Style: Procedure Phony*

6. Referencing Other Procedures
   - References to other sections should be made within the procedure step as follows:
     - (see 3.1.1 – Set up New Vendor)
     - References may be made to 4 or 5 digit procedures as well in the same fashion

3.1 Vendor Maintenance

3.1.1 Set up New Vendor

Responsibility: Static Data Associate (SDA)
Involved Parties: Corporate Sourcing
System(s): Peachtree
Procedures:

Corporate Sourcing is responsible for approving new vendors. After a new vendor is approved, they advise Accounts Payable of approval and payment terms. Accounts Payable is required to obtain a Tax Identification Number from all vendors.

1. Static Data Associate receives an email instruction (Exhibit 3.1.1a) from Corporate Sourcing to set up a new vendor and reviews email for completeness following up with Corporate Sourcing if necessary.
2. Call vendor contact for additional information and indicate information provided on email from Corporate Sourcing including:
   - Tax identification number (per Vendor Tax Reporting Policy)
   - Payment instructions
   - Ability to send invoice via PDF
   - Fax number
3. Complete fax cover sheet and form (Exhibit 3.1.1b) and fax to new vendor.
4. When vendor faxes completed form, SDA checks form for completeness and follows up with vendor contact if necessary.
5. SDA accesses Maintain Vendors screen on Peachtree (Exhibit 3.1.1c) and enters required data from email and New Vendor Form.
6. SDA sight checks the screen to verify that information has been entered accurately and completely.
7. SDA completes any necessary changes and releases the update in Peachtree.
8. SDA sets up a file for the new vendor and files paperwork in folder including:
   - Email from Corporate Sourcing
   - Completed fax form
9. File new vendor folder in Vendor File.

Link(s):
Vendor Tax Reporting Policy – www.ABCcorp.com/Policies/vendortaxpolicy.htm

6. Exhibits
  1. Procedures Section
     - Ensure reference in procedures corresponds to correct exhibit
       - Reference in procedures should be after the exhibit name as follows: (Exhibit 3.1.3.1A)
     - Reference exhibit to lowest level procedure (4 digit, 5 digit, etc.)

Corporate Sourcing is responsible for approving new vendors. After a new vendor is approved, they advise Accounts Payable of approval and payment terms. Accounts Payable is required to obtain a Tax Identification Number from all vendors.

1. Static Data Associate receives an email instruction (Exhibit 3.1.1a) from Corporate Sourcing to set up a new vendor and reviews email for completeness following up with Corporate Sourcing if necessary.
2. Call vendor contact for additional information and indicate information provided on email from Corporate Sourcing including:
   - Tax identification number (per Vendor Tax Reporting Policy)
   - Payment instructions
   - Ability to send invoice via PDF
   - Fax number
3. Complete fax cover sheet and form (Exhibit 3.1.1b) and fax to new vendor.

---

  2. Exhibits Section
     - Section Heading – 16 pt (*Style: Heading 1*)
     - Exhibit Listing
       - Format: number of exhibit, tab to 1.0, name of exhibit
       - 10 pt font

4.0 – Exhibits

3.1.1a	Vendor Setup Email Instruction
3.1.1b	New Vendor Form
3.1.1c	Peachtree Maintain Vendors Screen

     - Exhibits
       - Label in upper left corner of exhibit, 16 pt font

- Label should look as follows: Exhibit 3.2.1C
- Label on first page only of multi page exhibits
- Check that all exhibits in Exhibit Listing are present
- Check for clarity of exhibits

Exhibit 3.2.1C

Funds Transfer Request
Company ABC

Date: _____

Transfer Amount: _____
Debit Account: _____

---

7. Appendices
    1. Ensure all appendices are referenced to a procedure or at least mentioned in the Introduction/R&R
    2. Appendices are numbered 1 through . . .
    3. Introduction/R&R
        - Ensure reference in Introduction/R&R corresponds to correct appendix number
        - Reference in Introduction/R&R should be after the appendix name as follows: (Appendix 7)

1.4.1   Overview of Activities
Accounts Payable ensures that valid vendor invoices and employee expenses are paid timely for the US based division of Alpha Company. The group handles both electronic and check payments to vendors.

4. Procedures Section
  - Appendix reference in Link Box should look as follows:
    - Accounts Payable System Manual – Appendix 2
  - Ensure reference in Procedures section corresponds to correct appendix number

---

Link(s):
   Accounts Payable System Manual – Appendix 2

---

5. Appendices Section
  - Section Heading – 16 pt (*Style: Heading 1*)
  - Appendix Listing
    - Ensure listing and matrix contain the same items
    - Check numbering
    - 10 pt font

5.0 – Appendices

1. Tax/regulatory requirements
2. Accounts Payable System Manual

  - Appendices
    - Ensure that each appendix is behind the correct numbered tab (as per the listing)
    - Check that all appendices in Appendix Listing are present
    - Check for clarity of appendices
    - Check if any are printed two sided (to notify print shop)
8. Table of Contents
   1. Always update entire TOC before finalizing the manual
   2. Use the following styles for the headings in the document to be picked up in the TOC:
      - Section Headings – *Heading 1*

- 2 digit headings in Introduction/R&R – *Heading 1a*
- 3 digit headings in Introduction/R&R – *Heading 1b*
- 2 digit procedure heading – *Procedure 1a* (first 2 digit heading only)
  - Subsequent 2 digit procedure headings – *Procedure Phony* (not picked up in the TOC)
- 3 digit procedure heading – *Procedure 1b*
  - If 3 digit procedure heading goes on to multiple pages, subsequent pages use *Procedure Phony* style (not picked up in the TOC)

Post Duplication Review

When duplicated manuals are returned from Print Shop, Copying Company, or another employee, perform following checks before distributing the manuals.

1. Ensure that there is a color cover and spine in each binder

2. Ensure matrix is in front cover

3. Ensure that no pages are missing (look at page numbers)

4. Ensure no blank pages have been added

5. Ensure that all pages are in correct order

6. Ensure that all exhibits are present and in order, including the listing

7. Ensure that all appendices are present, including the listing

8. Ensure that all appendices are behind correct numbered tabs

9. Ensure any appendices that were to be two sided have been copied that way

10. Ensure that exhibits and appendices are clear and legible

11. Ensure that tabs are correct, clear and legible

Appendix 5: Sample Procedures with Screenshots

The following are examples of how you can use screenshots to supplement the procedures:

Example 1:

The screenshot follows each detailed procedure step.

Example 2:

The screenshot follows each detailed procedure step and has callouts with general information.

Example 3:

The screenshot follows each detailed procedure step and has callouts correlating with each step.

Example 4:

The screenshot follows each detailed procedure step and has callouts with numbers correlating with each step.

Example 1

The screenshot follows each detailed procedure step.

3.1   Manage Affirmations

3.1.1   Set Affirmation

Responsibility: Approver, Administrator
System(s):   FirmCover®
Procedures:

Affirmations ensure that FirmCover® users are aware of important policies and procedures in a manual.

1. Access FirmCover® program.
    - Enter Web address for FirmCover® instance in Internet browser.
    - Sign in using FirmCover® username and password.
2. In FirmCover® Home screen, click Management link.

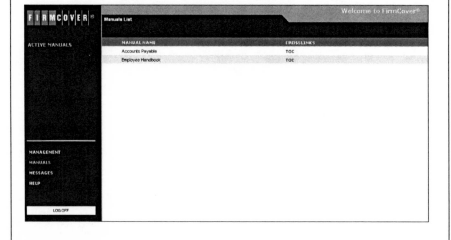

3.1   Manage Affirmations

3.1.1   Set Affirmation (Continued)

3. Click Manage Manuals link.

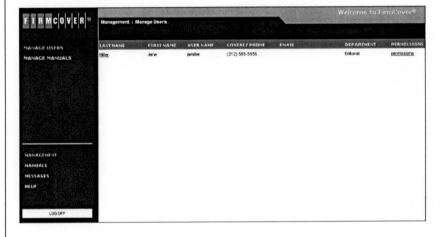

3.1   Manage Affirmations

3.1.1   Set Affirmation (Continued)

4. Find name of manual for which you want to set an affirmation, and then click
   Affirmation Settings link to the right of the manual name.

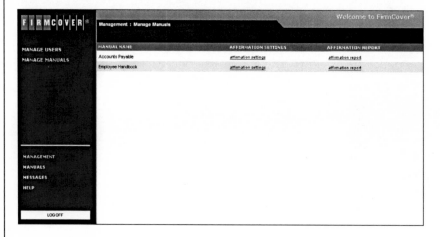

3.1   Manage Affirmations

3.1.1   Set Affirmation (Continued)

5. In Affirmations screen, enter affirmation information.
    1. Select checkbox to apply affirmation to manual.
    2. Enter affirmation text in Affirmation Content text box.
    3. Affirmation Creator and Affirmation Creation Time fields are updated automatically when affirmation is saved.
    4. Select expiration date for affirmation with Calendar tool.
    5. To send reminder, enter number of days in Send Reminder Email text box.
    6. Select users to whom affirmation applies. To select all users in a particular group, click the applicable link.

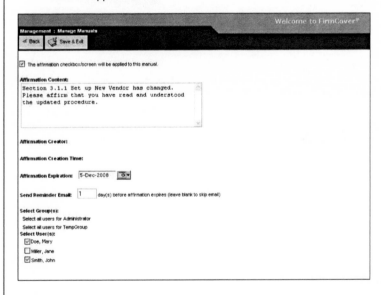

Example 2

The screenshot follows each detailed procedure step and has callouts with general information.

3.1 Manage Affirmations

3.1.1 Set Affirmation

Responsibility: Approver, Administrator
System(s): FirmCover®
Procedures:

Affirmations ensure that FirmCover® users are aware of important policies and procedures in a manual.

1. Access FirmCover® program.
   - Enter Web address for FirmCover® instance in Internet browser.
   - Sign in using FirmCover® username and password.
2. In FirmCover® Home screen, click Management link.

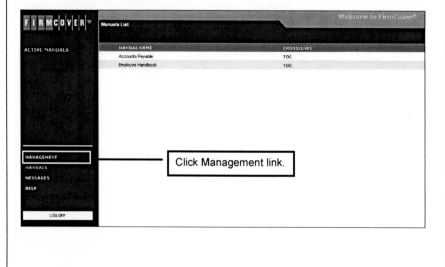

3.1   Manage Affirmations

3.1.1   Set Affirmation (Continued)

3. Click Manage Manuals link.

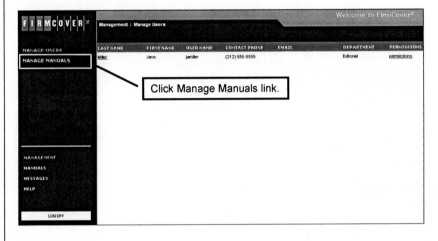

3.1   Manage Affirmations

3.1.1   Set Affirmation (Continued)

4. Find name of manual for which you want to set an affirmation, and then click Affirmation Settings link to the right of the manual name.

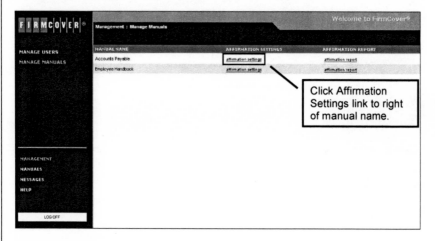

Click Affirmation Settings link to right of manual name.

3.1   Manage Affirmations

3.1.1   Set Affirmation (Continued)

5. In Affirmations screen, enter affirmation information.
    1. Select checkbox to apply affirmation to manual.
    2. Enter affirmation text in Affirmation Content text box.
    3. Affirmation Creator and Affirmation Creation Time fields are updated automatically when affirmation is saved.
    4. Select expiration date for affirmation with Calendar tool.
    5. To send reminder, enter number of days in Send Reminder Email text box.
    6. Select users to whom affirmation applies. To select all users in a particular group, click the applicable link.

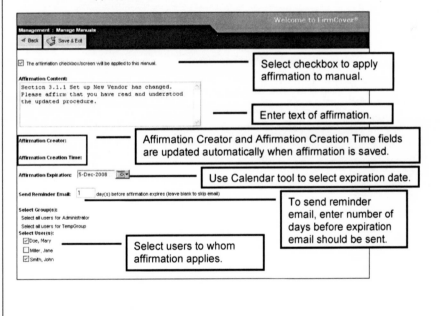

Example 3

The screenshot follows each detailed procedures step and has callouts correlating with each step.

3.1   Manage Affirmations

3.1.1   Set Affirmation

Responsibility: Approver, Administrator
System(s):   FirmCover®
Procedures:

Affirmations ensure that FirmCover® users are aware of important policies and procedures in a manual.

1. Access FirmCover® program.
    - Enter Web address for FirmCover® instance in Internet browser.
    - Sign in using FirmCover® username and password.
2. In FirmCover® Home screen, click Management link.

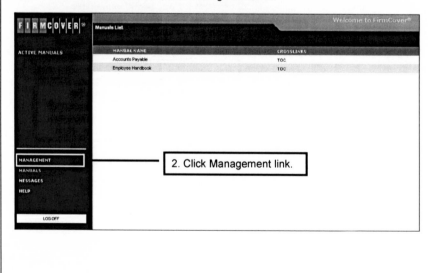

3.1   Manage Affirmations

3.1.1   Set Affirmation (Continued)

3. Click Manage Manuals link.

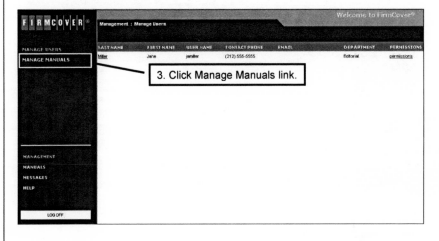

3.1   Manage Affirmations

3.1.1   Set Affirmation (Continued)

4. Find name of manual for which you want to set an affirmation, and then click Affirmation Settings link to the right of the manual name.

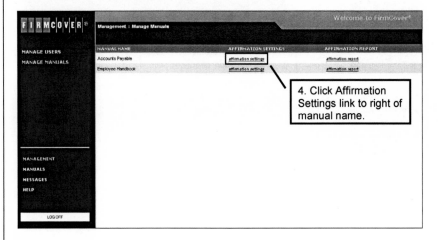

4. Click Affirmation Settings link to right of manual name.

3.1   Manage Affirmations

3.1.1   Set Affirmation (Continued)

5. In Affirmations screen, enter affirmation information.
    1. Select checkbox to apply affirmation to manual.
    2. Enter affirmation text in Affirmation Content text box.
    3. Affirmation Creator and Affirmation Creation Time fields are updated automatically when affirmation is saved.
    4. Select expiration date for affirmation with Calendar tool.
    5. To send reminder, enter number of days in Send Reminder Email text box.
    6. Select users to whom affirmation applies. To select all users in a particular group, click the applicable link.

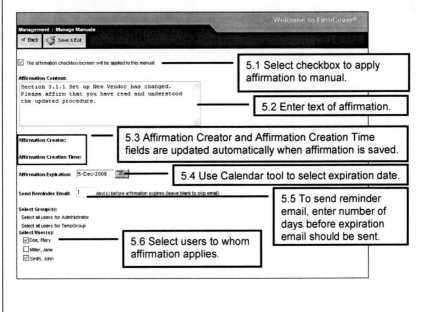

5.1 Select checkbox to apply affirmation to manual.

5.2 Enter text of affirmation.

5.3 Affirmation Creator and Affirmation Creation Time fields are updated automatically when affirmation is saved.

5.4 Use Calendar tool to select expiration date.

5.5 To send reminder email, enter number of days before expiration email should be sent.

5.6 Select users to whom affirmation applies.

Example 4

The screenshot follows each detailed procedure step and has callouts with numbers correlating with each step.

3.1   Manage Affirmations

3.1.1   Set Affirmation

Responsibility: Approver, Administrator
System(s):   FirmCover®
Procedures:

Affirmations ensure that FirmCover® users are aware of important policies and procedures in a manual.

1. Access FirmCover® program.
   - Enter Web address for FirmCover® instance in Internet browser.
   - Sign in using FirmCover® username and password.
2. In FirmCover® Home screen, click Management link.

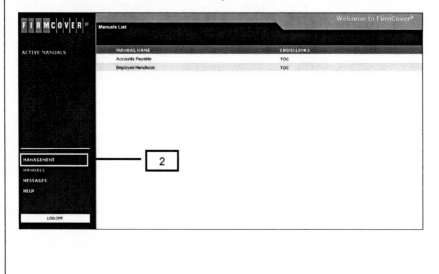

3.1   Manage Affirmations

3.1.1   Set Affirmation (Continued)

3. Click Manage Manuals link.

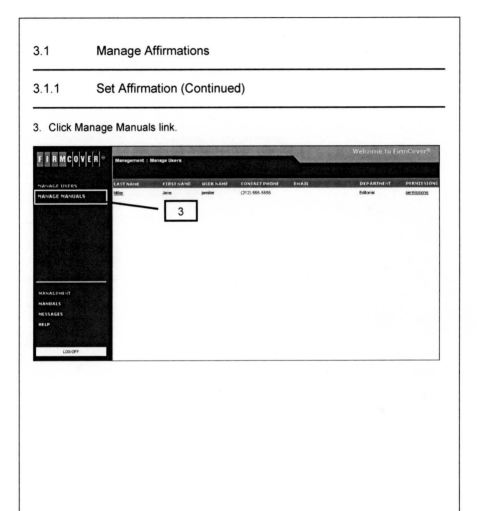

3.1 Manage Affirmations

3.1.1 Set Affirmation (Continued)

4. Find name of manual for which you want to set an affirmation, and then click Affirmation Settings link to the right of the manual name.

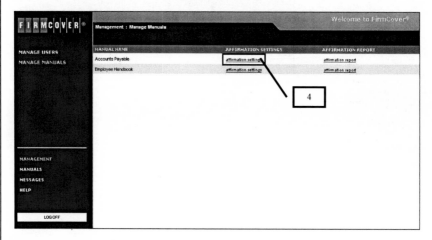

3.1   Manage Affirmations

3.1.1   Set Affirmation (Continued)

5. In Affirmations screen, enter affirmation information.
    1. Select checkbox to apply affirmation to manual.
    2. Enter affirmation text in Affirmation Content text box.
    3. Affirmation Creator and Affirmation Creation Time fields are updated automatically when affirmation is saved.
    4. Select expiration date for affirmation with Calendar tool.
    5. To send reminder, enter number of days in Send Reminder Email text box.
    6. Select users to whom affirmation applies. To select all users in a particular group, click the applicable link.

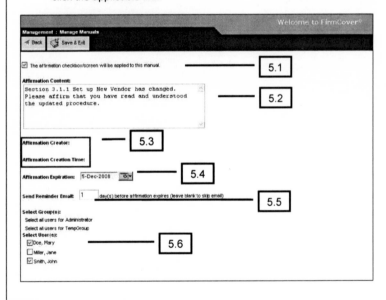

Index